Arms Watch

SIPRI Report on the First Year of the UN Register of Conventional Arms

sipri

Stockholm International Peace Research Institute

Pipers väg 28, S-170 73 Solna, Sweden
Cable: SIPRI
Telephone: 46 8/655 97 00
Telefax: 46 8/655 97 33

Arms Watch

SIPRI Report on the First Year of the UN Register of Conventional Arms

SIPRI Research Report No. 6

Edward J. Laurance, Siemon T. Wezeman and Herbert Wulf

OXFORD UNIVERSITY PRESS
1993

Oxford University Press, Walton Street, Oxford OX2 6DP
Oxford New York Toronto
Delhi Bombay Calcutta Madras Karachi
Kuala Lumpur Singapore Hong Kong Tokyo
Nairobi Dar es Salaam Cape Town
Melbourne Auckland Madrid
and associated companies in
Berlin Ibadan

Oxford is a trade mark of Oxford University Press

Published in the United States
by Oxford University Press Inc., New York

British Library Cataloguing in Publication Data
Data available
Library of Congress Cataloging in Publication Data
Laurance, Edward J.
Arms watch: SIPRI report on the first year of the UN register of conventional arms
/ Edward J. Laurance, Siemon T. Wezeman and Herbert Wulf.
— (SIPRI research report; no. 6) Includes index.
1. Arms control. I. Wezeman, Siemon T. II. Wulf, Herbert, 1939–
III. Stockholm International Peace Research Institute. IV. Title. V. Series.
JX1974.L33 1993 327.1'74'dc20 93–36596
ISBN 0–19–829179–5
ISBN 0–19–829177–9 (Pbk.)
Typeset and originated by Stockholm International Peace Research Institute
Printed in Great Britain
on acid-free paper by
Biddles Ltd., Guildford and King's Lynn

Contents

Annexes

Foreword

Whether or not the United Nations Register of Conventional Arms could have been established earlier, the end of the cold war era made it possible for governments to release substantive information about arms transfers.

The fact that, for over 25 years, *SIPRI Yearbooks* have provided information to the public regarding arms trade, based on public sources, at least to some extent influenced the decision to establish the UN Register of Conventional Arms in December 1991. The start of this Register marks a specific stage in the process of bringing arms trade under international control. It is natural, then, that SIPRI should present the first assessment of the activities of the new institution.

In preparing this report the authors owe a particular debt to the individuals who 25 years ago had the foresight to establish the SIPRI arms transfer data base and the tenacity and expertise to maintain and develop it. The data collection remains an important resource for the independent evaluation of government reporting on arms transfers.

The arms transfers project is SIPRI's oldest continuous research project, dating back to 1967. Its central focus is a data base containing information on deliveries of major conventional weapons since 1950. When governments decided to establish an official body of data on exports and imports of weapons in seven defined categories, it was of more than passing interest.

Without the reduction in obsessive secrecy relating to security matters, progress in limiting and reducing conventional arms in Europe would have been difficult. Further development and expansion of the UN Register of Conventional Arms may be steps towards conventional arms control outside Europe.

While the governments of the major powers will always insist on intelligence gathered by national means as the basis for policy, the unilateral public release of government-generated data is a political act. Data are unlikely to be falsified but will be presented in a way which supports the policy preferences of the agency where it originated. Neither this information nor coercive data collection of the type enforced on Iraq can promote dialogue between states.

An agreed body of official data is a prerequisite for dialogue on security matters, and a realistic picture of weapon acquisitions can only be constructed by governments on a co-operative basis. Otherwise a government wanting to stall discussions can easily avoid dealing with substantive issues by questioning the numbers.

The research on which this report is based owes its results to the commitment and effort of the authors—Edward J. Laurance, Siemon T. Wezeman and Herbert Wulf, the initiator of the work. They have collected and analysed a great deal of not always easily available data and information, compared them with the data at SIPRI's disposal, and in this report offer their estimates, conclusions and postulates.

Connie Wall shouldered a tremendous responsibility for this report; she edited the manuscript in a short period of time and co-ordinated the work of the authors, who were working in three different locations. She contributed immensely to completing the report in a fashion that makes it both scholarly and good reading.

Project secretary Cynthia Loo assisted the project with characteristic efficiency.

Adam Daniel Rotfeld
Director

Preface

The United Nations Register of Conventional Arms can be evaluated from at least three perspectives: What does it tell us about the nature of multilateral negotiations after the cold war? What does it tell us about government attitudes towards information concerning national security? What does it tell us about the international arms trade?

The UN Register is not an academic construction but the product of an inter-governmental process. The decision to seek a voluntary, global agreement suggests that governments still see merit in multilateralism in spite of the trend towards introspection among the great powers.

Unlike the government-to-government information exchange within the CSCE, governments decided to open the UN Register to public scrutiny. Why they took this uncharacteristic step remains unknown.

The least interesting aspect of the UN Register is probably what it reveals about the international arms trade. The Register confirms what was already known: that there was little trade in major weapon systems in 1992 and what there was was highly concentrated among a small group of exporters and importers.

The limited scope of reporting underlines that governments are still sensitive about releasing information related to military capability, and critics should recognize that the choice is not between a mandatory, detailed register and a voluntary, limited register but between a voluntary, limited register and no register at all. However, the resolution founding the UN Register requires its expansion, which may increase the amount of data included and disaggregate that data to help in evaluating patterns of arms procurement. This process cannot move more quickly than governments are prepared to let it, and governments may need several years before they are satisfied that no negative developments have resulted from the current UN Register. Further development should be seen as a long-term process with the aim of establishing the UN Register as a permanent United Nations activity.

This report represents one element of what SIPRI hopes will be continuous collaboration with the UN and member governments in developing transparency in armaments.

Ian Anthony
Arms Production and Arms Transfers Project Leader
September 1993

Acronyms and abbreviations

AAV(G)	Anti-aircraft vehicle (gun-armed)
AAV(M)	Anti-aircraft vehicle (missile-armed)
ac	Aircraft
ACDA	(US) Arms Control and Disarmament Agency
ACV	Armoured combat vehicle
ADATS	Air defence and anti-tank system
AEW	Airborne early-warning (system)
AEW&C	Airborne early-warning and control
AIFV	Armoured infantry fighting vehicle
ALARM	Air-launched anti-radar missile
AMRAAM	Advanced medium-range air-to-air missile
APC	Armoured personnel carrier
ARV	Armoured recovery vehicle
ASW	Anti-submarine warfare
Atk Helo	Attack helicopter
CATT	Conventional Arms Trade Talks
Cbt Acft	Combat aircraft
CD	Conference on Disarmament
CDS	Coastal defence system
CFE	Conventional Armed Forces in Europe
CIWS	Close-in weapon system
COCOM	Co-ordinating Committee (on Multilateral Export Controls)
CRS	Congressional Research Service (US Library of Congress)
CSCE	Conference on Security and Co-operation in Europe
CWC	Chemical Weapons Convention
Elint	Electronic intelligence
FMS	Foreign Military Sales (USA)
GATT	General Agreement on Tariffs and Trade
grd attack	Ground attack
incl	Including/includes
LAV	Light armoured vehicle
LCA	Large-calibre artillery (system)
M	Missile
MCM	Mine countermeasures (ship)
mis	Missile

M/Ml	Missile and missile launcher
MLRS	Multiple-launch rocket system
MRL	Multiple rocket launcher
MTCR	Missile Technology Control Regime
NATO	North Atlantic Treaty Organization
NP	Non-participation
NR	Non-reporting *or* Not reported
ODA	(UN) Office for Disarmament Affairs
P5	Permanent Five (members of UN Security Council)
RAM	Rolling airframe missile
Recce	Reconnaissance
SAM	Surface-to-air missile
SAMS	Surface-to-air missile system
ShAM	Ship-to-air missile
ShShM	Ship-to-ship missile
SSM	Surface-to-surface missile
START	Strategic Arms Reductions Treaty
SuShM	Submarine-to-ship missile
sys	System
TLE	Treaty-limited equipment
UAE	United Arab Emirates
UN	United Nations
UNSCOM	UN Special Commission on Iraq
VLS	Vertical launch system

Conventions in the tables

. .	Data not available or not applicable
–	Negligible figure (< 0.5) or none
( )	Uncertain data or SIPRI estimate

1. Executive summary

Government reports for calendar year 1992 on the transfer of major conventional weapons, in seven categories, have been submitted to the United Nations Secretary-General in compliance with General Assembly Resolution 46/36 L (1991) and the report of the UN Secretary-General (1992). This is the first time since the League of Nations' *Statistical Year-book* on the trade in arms, munitions and implements of war, published from 1925 to 1938, that official statistics on the transfer of arms have been collected on a global scale. What are the results of the first year of reporting to the UN Register of Conventional Arms? What new information was made public and what already publicly known information was confirmed?

1. Of the UN member states and observer states invited,[1] 78 governments responded to the Secretary-General's request: 24 countries reported arms exports, 37 countries reported imports, 41 nil reports on exports were submitted, 30 nil reports on imports were submitted, 31 countries submitted explanations in a *note verbale*, and 34 countries submitted background information.

2. Most arms exporters, but only two-thirds of all importers, reported to the United Nations, which can be seen using SIPRI data on arms transfers for 1992 as a base line. These exporters account for 98 per cent of the total value of exports of major conventional weapon systems and the importers for about 65 per cent of the imports.

3. The significant number of countries which did not report to the UN Register can most likely be explained by the fact that in 1992 they conducted no arms trade in the seven Register weapon categories, although all UN members, including those that did not transfer arms, were asked to report.

4. Key groups of arms importers did not report, particularly governments in the Middle East and Asia.

5. Libya, embargoed by the United Nations, Egypt and Israel were the only Middle Eastern countries that reported. Libya submitted a 'nil report' on arms transfers; Egypt and Israel reported both exports

---

[1] The Secretary-General's request was sent to 186 countries: all the UN member states (184 as of Aug. 1993) and two observer states (the Holy See [Vatican City] and Switzerland).

and imports. Among the key countries in Asia that did not report were Bangladesh, Indonesia, North Korea and Thailand.[2]

6. As a result of the NATO 'cascade' of arms transfers following the 1990 Treaty on Conventional Armed Forces in Europe (CFE),[3] Greece and Turkey are major importers of conventional weapons.

7. The United States held the dominant position in the export of conventional weapons and was the major exporter in several of the seven weapon categories. Germany was the second largest supplier, with arms exports in each of the seven weapon categories.

8. Critical and previously unknown information on arms transfers involving the seven UN Register weapon categories was made public by the Register, mainly in land systems. Examples include: Italy, transfer of artillery to Nigeria; Romania, armour and artillery to Moldova; China, artillery to Iran; and France, artillery to Saudi Arabia.

9. Some critical and publicly known arms transfers were *not* reported by countries participating in the UN Register. A 'grey area' is being created by broad Register definitions for attack helicopters and combat aircraft. As a result, some countries chose not to report systems that were publicly reported as meeting the UN Register definitions. Examples include: Switzerland, transfer of trainer aircraft to Thailand; Brazil, trainer aircraft to Colombia; Czechoslovakia, trainer aircraft to Egypt; and the USA, helicopters to the Philippines.

10. The total number of *arms transfers or deals* reported to the UN Register in all categories is greater than that reported in the SIPRI register. SIPRI reports 418 separate deals involving weapons falling within the seven UN Register categories, of which 78 are for licensed production and 197 are deals for weapons on order but for which no deliveries were recorded for 1992, leaving 143 entries on deliveries of weapons covered by the UN Register. This can be compared to 192 actual deals in the UN Register.

11. The number of *weapon systems (items)* reported to the UN Register, by exporter, importer or both, is in some weapon categories significantly higher than reported in the SIPRI register, as shown below.

---

[2] Taiwan, a major arms-importing country but not a UN member state, was not asked to report to the UN Register.

[3] The CFE Treaty ceiling on certain weapon categories has led to a 'cascade' within NATO: weapons that must be withdrawn from the Treaty area are—in accordance with the Treaty—'cascaded' or transferred to other NATO countries which in turn have agreed to destroy older equipment. The main suppliers are the US forces in Europe and Germany.

Category	No. items, UN Register	No. items, SIPRI register
Tanks	1 733	1 964
Armoured combat vehicles	1 625	618
Large-calibre artillery systems	1 676	564
Combat aircraft	270	447
Attack helicopters	40	63
Warships	33	14
Missiles/missile launchers	67 838	1 590

12. The above comparison of both deals and items confirms that in certain areas, such as combat aircraft and helicopters, the SIPRI data reveal that the UN Register does not report all transfers which fall in the agreed UN Register categories. It also should be noted that because of the different structure of the two registers, SIPRI makes transparent a great deal of important information on the arms trade which is not covered by the UN Register. On the other hand, the UN Register revealed some previously unknown transfers, as well as adding important new information on the scale and timing of transfers about which only general information was known. It also officially confirmed much that was already known.

13. Thirty-one countries used the description and/or comments columns of the forms to provide details on the type or model of the weapon systems transferred or added comments to explain the transfers.

14. In most cases, suppliers and recipients did not co-ordinate their returns. Only 51 of the 192 entries matched. With regard to the cross-checking function of the UN Register (a comparison of the entries of exporters and importers), 126 entries (or 66 per cent) could not be verified since one of the parties did not participate in the UN Register or did not report the particular transfers; 17 entries gave conflicting information on the number of items reported; and 51 entries matched.

15. Focusing on the number of items rather than entries, 90 per cent of the tanks reported, 32 per cent of the armoured combat vehicles, 48 per cent of the large-calibre artillery, 67 per cent of the combat aircraft, 43 per cent of the attack helicopters, 15 per cent of the warships, and 13 per cent of the missiles and missile launchers could be verified through cross-checking. While the lack of confirmed information on arms transfers is due in part to non-reporting, many of the differences are likely to be due to differing procedural approaches by the various governments regarding the precise definition of the weapon categories, delivery dates or assumptions about control of ownership.

2. Introduction

I. The rationale for this book

Controlling the trade in arms through international or multilateral mechanisms has consistently been a non-starter. This was particularly true during the cold war since the two major protagonists, the United States and the Soviet Union, exported 80–90 per cent of the value of the arms trade. With the end of the cold war, the potential for dealing with the negative consequences of the arms trade increased significantly. The 1990 Iraqi invasion of Kuwait created a historic consensus that the transfer of conventional arms can lead to excessive and destabilizing accumulations and led to the creation in 1991 of the United Nations Register of Conventional Arms. This book chronicles and evaluates the first year of the UN Register: it compares the data reported to the Register with arms trade data published by SIPRI and examines the implications of expanding the UN Register into an effective tool for dampening the negative consequences of this trade.

By 25 September 1993, 78 states (77 UN member states and one observer state) had submitted data to the UN on their arms exports and imports for 1992.[1] While this Register has been hailed as historic, it is not the first attempt at such an exercise in making official arms transfer data transparent to the public. The League of Nations published such data from 1925 to 1938, and for the past 25 years SIPRI has published its own annual arms trade register in the *SIPRI Yearbook* based on public sources of information.[2]

Despite a great deal of effort since the 1991 Persian Gulf War to develop national and multilateral arms trade control regimes, only the UN Register has evolved as a multilateral mechanism with the potential to deal with the negative consequences of the arms trade. In the autumn of 1993, data submitted as part of the UN Register process were made public in a report from the UN Secretary-General. With

[1] After completion of the manuscript for this report, Mauritius filed a nil report, bringing the total to 79 states as of end-Sep. 1993.
[2] The latest SIPRI register was published in 1993: 'Register of the trade in and licensed production of major conventional weapons in industrialized and developing countries, 1992', *SIPRI Yearbook 1993: World Armaments and Disarmament* (Oxford University Press: Oxford, 1993), appendix 10C, pp. 483–518.

the first year of the Register now complete,[3] it is appropriate to assess
the first year's experience, especially in the light of the very well
established and utilized data in the SIPRI register. How many states
reported and what was the level of transparency of the data? How did
the cross-checking between exporters and importers work? How did
these data compare with those of SIPRI? Is there a continuing need
for arms trade data from SIPRI and other institutions which utilize
publicly available sources?

In addition to the analysis, the book includes three annexes.
Annexe 1 presents data from the actual returns submitted to the
United Nations by those states participating in the UN Register for
1992. Annexe 2 contains the SIPRI register data for 1992. In
annexe 3, excerpts from the major descriptions and assessments of the
UN Register process which had been published as of 1 June 1993 are
assembled. They are referred to often in the chapters and also serve as
a resource for those wishing for more detailed assessments of the
history, philosophy and rationale of the UN Register as well as its
potential for future development.

This book is designed to serve as a major resource for those
researchers, policy makers and members of the public involved with
evaluating and developing the utility of the UN Register as a tool for
dealing with the arms trade and its consequences.

II. Previous efforts to register the arms trade

The concept of an arms register—the publication and making transparent of data on those items of military equipment deemed most
related to and responsible for armed conflict and its consequences—
dates back to the aftermath of World War I. The Covenant of the
League of Nations, adopted in 1919, included an article on arms
transfers: '. . . the Members of the League . . . will entrust the League
with the general supervision of the trade in arms and ammunition
with the countries in which the control of this traffic is necessary in
the common interest' (Article 23, para. d).

In 1925 the first *Statistical Year-book* of the League of Nations was
published, showing the values of arms imports and imports based on

---

[3] A deadline of 30 Apr. 1993 was originally set for submission of data, but since the
Register is voluntary states may submit data throughout 1993. This book evaluates the UN
Register using data submitted as of 25 Sep. 1993.

official national statistics. The publication of these arms trade data continued through 1938, the final volume covering 60 countries and 64 colonies, protectorates and mandated territories.[4] With the onset of World War II, this register ceased to operate.

It was to be some 30 years until SIPRI decided to return to this effort at making arms trade data transparent in the form of a register, albeit with information from non-governmental sources. In the first *SIPRI Yearbook*,[5] SIPRI published the first arms trade register and the Institute has maintained it ever since. SIPRI had some competition in this field, including the Massachusetts Institute of Technology (MIT) project on arms transfers to the developing world and the data published by US Government agencies such as the Arms Control and Disarmament Agency (ACDA), the Defense Security Assistance Agency and the Library of Congress Congressional Research Service (CRS).[6] None except SIPRI published data that were timely (i.e., data for the previous year) and relevant for assessing the negative political and military consequences of the arms trade, that is, numbers of items of equipment of a specific type and model. SIPRI continued to refine its valuation techniques and enhance its sources of public information over the years and, at the time of the two seminal events of the Persian Gulf War and the end of the cold war, had become an indispensable source of data for those charged with analysing the effects of the arms trade on conflict, political influence and economic development.

III. The Persian Gulf War and arms trade control

The 1990 Iraqi invasion of Kuwait and the allied response in 1991 created an unprecedented international consensus that the accumulation of advanced conventional weapon systems can be a major factor in the outbreak, conduct and termination of armed conflict. Combined with the end of the cold war and the decline of the military threat from the Soviet Union, the result was a well-documented increase in the attention paid to the proliferation of destabilizing and dangerous

---

[4] *Study on Ways and Means of Promoting Transparency in International Transfers of Conventional Arms, Report of the Secretary-General,* UN General Assembly document A/46/301, 9 Sep. 1991.

[5] *SIPRI Yearbook of World Armaments and Disarmament 1968/69* (Almqvist & Wiksell: Stockholm, 1969), section ID.

[6] For a comprehensive treatment of arms transfer data sources, see Laurance, E. J., *The International Arms Trade* (Lexington Books: New York, 1992), chapter 2.

accumulations of weapon systems as a major threat to international stability.

Many arms supplier states tightened up their national export control systems. There were policy proposals from many quarters to develop multilateral and international control mechanisms designed to prevent a repetition of the Iraqi situation. The five permanent members of the UN Security Council (who were, for most of the 1980s, the five leading exporters of arms) began meeting in July 1991 to develop some multilateral restraints on destabilizing arms transfers in the so-called P5 Talks. However, these traditional arms trade control approaches soon fell victim to the realities that have always existed, as the major suppliers found it difficult to agree on a process that would define a transfer as destabilizing prior to its delivery. Furthermore, when the end of the cold war produced rapidly declining orders for domestic defence production, pressure from the defence industries was clearly working against any movement towards national or international arms export controls.

IV. The United Nations Register of Conventional Arms[7]

Despite the initial post-Persian Gulf War enthusiasm in some quarters for actual regulation and restraint of the arms trade, by the spring of 1991 transparency began to be seen as the first, minimal step that could be taken. Much of the impetus for the idea came from the degree of transparency, albeit unintended, which emerged from the lists of firms and the items they exported to Iraq produced by investigative reporting. As states began to publish more information on their exports, expectations began to rise and the outline of an international arms register, a non-starter just a few years before, began to take shape.

During the Persian Gulf War, a UN study on the arms trade was under way.[8] In 1990 the chairman of that group, Italian Ambassador Eugenio Plaja, in a background paper delivered to the UN symposium on transparency in Florence, felt that an international arms register

---

[7] This section is based on Laurance, E. J. and Wulf, H., 'The continued quest for transparency in armaments: quantity versus utility of information', paper presented at the United Nations Symposium on Transparency in Armaments, Florence, Italy, 29 Mar.–1 Apr. 1993.

[8] *Study on Ways and Means* (note 4).

was premature: 'A general register to be kept by the United Nations is often mentioned, but it might prove somewhat difficult to establish in the first instance. In this case, let us not overlook or consider as unimportant more limited measures, such as proposing methodological models to be followed on a regional or bilateral level . . .'.[9] By September 1991, when the final report was published, such caution no longer existed. In his foreword to the report, the UN Secretary-General stated: 'A practical recommendation made by the group of experts, to which I attach the greatest importance, is the creation of a universal and non-discriminatory register of arms transfers under the auspices of the United Nations'.[10]

Concurrent with the study, governments of the European Community and Japan put forward formal proposals for the establishment of a Register of International Arms Transfers. Only after stiff resistance from some key developing states did the final resolution establishing the UN Register incorporate language expanding the concept of a register beyond trade to include procurement through national production and military holdings and the prospect that technology transfers and weapons of mass destruction would also be part of the Register. The resolution, entitled Transparency in Armaments (Resolution 46/36 L), passed in the General Assembly by a vote of 150–0 on 9 December 1991, with Cuba and Iraq abstaining and China and Syria not participating. The Register was put into operation on 1 January 1992, and in April 1993 member states began voluntarily submitting to the UN data on transfers of weapons and background information on military holdings, procurement through national production and relevant policies for the calendar year 1992.[11]

A major element of the philosophy of the UN Register is that states need to gain confidence that registering and evaluating data will be done in a manner which involves all states and is non-discriminatory. In the words of Ambassador Hendrik Wagenmakers, one of the architects of the Register and the chairman of the Panel of Governmental Technical Experts which developed its operating procedures, the

---

[9] Plaja, E., 'The urgency of facing the problem of international arms transfers', *Transparency in International Arms Transfers,* Topical Papers 3 (United Nations Department [now Office] for Disarmament Affairs: New York, 1990), p. 71.

[10] *Study on Ways and Means* (note 4).

[11] For a description of the development of the UN Register, see Wulf, H., 'The United Nations Register of Conventional Arms', *SIPRI Yearbook 1993* (note 2), appendix 10F, pp. 533–44 (see annexe 3 for an excerpt from this appendix).

Register is a 'concrete expression' of this theme of transparency, which is designed 'to reduce the causes of dangerous misperceptions of another country's intentions and, where possible, to build partnership and trust'.[12]

It is also important to stress that the UN Register as it evolved is not an arms control mechanism. The language in the first paragraph of Resolution 46/36 L (1991) establishing the Register refers to 'excessive and destabilizing arms build-ups pos[ing] a threat to national, regional and international peace and security, particularly by aggravating tensions and conflict situations'. Further on in this resolution, arms transfers are described as having 'potentially negative effects on the progress of . . . peaceful social and economic development' and the need is expressed to create 'a world free from the scourge of war and the burden of armaments'.

The UN Register exists as only a first step in which governments can submit data which can be formally addressed in UN forums and form the basis for consultations between states. The Register has no traditional verification mechanism, save the fact that the identical arms transfer should be reported by both the importer and exporter states. This creates a situation in which a state hesitant to report an arms transfer may be faced with the return of the state at the other end of the deal. It is, however, the first instrument in place in the new UN effort to link disarmament with international peace and security. Given the recent resurgence of the UN Security Council's role in peace-keeping and its identification of weapon proliferation as a major threat to international security, there is some optimism that this approach can work.

V. The continuing problems of defining and measuring arms transfers

Efforts to control and study the international arms trade have been fraught with controversies regarding the definition and measurement of arms transfers. For example, at the national level, where all control of the arms trade has existed up to this point, any changes to lists of commodities to be controlled create controversy. The formation and

---

[12] Wagenmakers, H., 'The UN Register of Conventional Arms: a new instrument for cooperative security', *Arms Control Today*, Apr. 1993, p. 16 (see annexe 3 for an excerpt from this article).

adjustment of national arms export control policies and procedures mainly concern issues of definition and measurement. At the multilateral level, the conflicts among the members of COCOM (Coordinating Committee on Multilateral Export Controls) regarding which items were to be restricted for export to the USSR are well-documented. Further, when the USA and the USSR were exploring the control of the arms trade in the 1978–79 Conventional Arms Trade Talks (CATT), both sides found it difficult to agree on items to be controlled. In the most recent multilateral arms trade control effort, the now stalled Security Council P5 Talks, some agreement was reached on categories of weapons to be discussed, but the talks foundered when they could not agree on an operational definition for the timing of arms transfers to be controlled (e.g., orders or deliveries).

Definitional issues are not restricted to governments. Academics who address the arms trade are forced to use data which are developed using different units of analysis, categories of systems, units of measurement, and so on. The development of the SIPRI register of the arms trade involved a series of methodological decisions as to the operational definition and measurement of an arms transfer.[13] It is not surprising therefore that in the development of the UN Register these same methodological problems plagued its architects, developers and administrators in the First Committee (Political and Security, including disarmament) of the General Assembly, the Panel of Governmental Technical Experts, national governments charged with submitting the data and the UN Secretariat charged with administering the Register.

One of the first major issues to be decided for the UN Register was whether the data would involve orders or deliveries. The decision to use delivery data from the previous calendar year reflects a basic philosophical pillar of the Register, namely, 'excessive and destabilizing' accumulations cannot be so judged except in context and after the fact. This reflects the futility of most attempts to control arms transfers by stopping the sale prior to delivery (e.g., CATT and the P5 Talks) and the recognition that the arms trade is both legal and legitimate.

A second issue concerned defining when and where a transfer occurs for the purpose of reporting to the Register. General Assembly

[13] For a thorough review of these issues, see Laurance (note 6), chapter 2.

Resolution 46/32 L defined a transfer as items 'imported into or exported from [a state's] territory'. It also states that '[a]rms "exports and imports" represent in the present resolution, including its annex, all forms of arms transfers under terms of grant, credit, barter or cash.' It was also specified that the Register would record only those transfers made by governments, ruling out illicit arms sales.

A third general issue concerned the types of item to be included in the Register. If the goal of the Register is to monitor the buildup of military capability so that it may be scrutinized by the international community, some states felt that it should include weapons of mass destruction and the transfer of technology. It was decided to postpone both these issues by assigning the topic to the Conference on Disarmament (CD), whose report will be considered by a group of governmental technical experts who are charged in the resolution with considering these and other issues in 1994 (hereafter referred to as the 1994 Group). The CD will also consider adding military holdings (inventories) and procurement through national production to the Register and will submit its findings to the 1994 Group.

The 1991 resolution included an annex with seven categories of weapons—battle tanks, armoured combat vehicles, large-calibre artillery systems, combat aircraft, attack helicopters, warships, and missiles or missile systems. The rationale for choosing these categories further defines the basic philosophy of the Register: the 'focus is on weapons indispensable for surprise attacks and large-scale military actions. These weapon systems are relatively easy to identify, define, record and monitor'.[14] The first five categories are close to the categories developed for the 1990 Treaty on Conventional Armed Forces in Europe (CFE), while warships and missiles or missile launchers were added. Since the focus is on offensive military capability, the UN Register does not address the monetary value of transfers, despite the fact that the resolution mentions in several places that military expenditures detract from social and economic development. Also, by focusing on major end-items, the Register philosophy is further defined to exclude spare parts, components and upgrade kits that most certainly can add to a country's military capability. However, they would be difficult to monitor and therefore violated the dominant philosophy of creating a Register which most countries could contribute to during the formative first two years.

[14] Wagenmakers (note 12), p. 16.

Once the resolution was passed, it was up to a Panel of Governmental Technical Experts from 17 countries to develop the procedures for the actual operation of the Register. Most of the work of this Panel focused on the above-mentioned issues of definition and measurement. For example, in the final report to the Secretary-General of 14 August 1992, five paragraphs are devoted to further clarifying the definition of an international arms transfer. As only one example, the report makes the point that '[i]nternational arms transfers involve, in addition to the physical movement of equipment into or from national territory, the transfer of title to and control over the equipment'. The report gives several illustrative examples. As to when a transfer becomes effective, no consensus operational definition could be agreed to, given the variety of national approaches. States are therefore urged to report data 'in conformity with their respective national criteria used to define when a transfer becomes effective'.[15]

As for the categories, Resolution 46/36 L (para. 8) gave the Panel the mandate to 'make any adjustments to the annex', where the original seven categories and their definitions appear. A significant amount of the Panel discussion concerned changes to these definitions and the addition of categories. The basic focus of the Register, that is, offensive and destabilizing weapon systems, was often cited by those pushing for the addition or elimination of categories; but a consensus operational meaning of 'offensive' eluded the Panel, as it has most analysts throughout history. As for 'adjusting' the category definitions, several adjustments were made. For example, in the missile and missile launcher category, ground-to-air missiles were excluded as being 'non-offensive', although this rationale is never formally cited. Surface-to-air missiles mounted on ships, however, are to be registered. In the warship category, language was added so that exports and imports of missile-armed attack craft were to registered. Torpedoes were also added.[16] In the end, the Panel retained the seven basic categories, leaving to the 1994 Group the assignment to address further changes in the categories.

The disparity in reporting data, as shown in chapter 3, indicates that despite the work of the Panel there is still disagreement in national procedures regarding the definition and measurement of international

---

[15] *Report on the Register of Conventional Arms, Report of the Secretary-General*, UN General Assembly document A/47/342, 14 Aug. 1992 (see annexe 3).

[16] For a complete description of these changes, see Wulf (note 11).

arms transfers and categories of weapon systems. No doubt the 1994 Group will use the actual returns from the first two years to further operationally define an international arms transfer as well as the weapon categories. Also, it should be noted that much of the data reported by governments in the UN Register for 1992 was presumed by many to be public, but the public data are also subject to the same definitional and measurement problems, especially since much of the public data comes from government sources. The public data most comparable to those submitted by governments are those produced by SIPRI. Before turning to an assessment of the SIPRI data in chapter 4, their relationship to the UN Register is briefly discussed.

VI. SIPRI and the UN Register

The establishment of the UN Register in 1991 coincided with the 25th anniversary of SIPRI, but the UN Register is much more closely related to the work of SIPRI than a mere coincidence in timing might suggest.

SIPRI's long-term efforts in reporting trends in the trade in major conventional weapons were instrumental in the establishment of the UN Register. The experience of the SIPRI arms transfer research [was] taken into consideration, and [one of the authors of this book, Herbert Wulf] served as a consultant to the UN Panel of Governmental Technical Experts in 1992 in his capacity as Leader of the SIPRI arms transfers research project.[17]

In the first few sessions of the Panel of Governmental Technical Experts in the spring of 1992, the Panel members were briefed on how SIPRI collects data and in what form. Furthermore, Prvoslav Davinic, the present Director of the UN Office for Disarmament Affairs (ODA), which is responsible for the administration of the Register, was one of the authors of the still classic SIPRI study on the arms trade with the Third World.[18] SIPRI's experience and status also came to the fore during the four UN-sponsored regional workshops held on the UN Register in Tokyo, Buenos Aires, Warsaw and Florence in January–March 1993. At each of these workshops a researcher from SIPRI made a presentation to the participants (the government officials charged with assembling their country's arms

[17] See footnote 5 in Wulf (note 11), p. 533.
[18] SIPRI, *The Arms Trade With the Third World* (Almqvist & Wiksell: Stockholm, 1971).

trade data and completing the forms) regarding SIPRI's data on the arms deliveries which had occurred in 1992, according to the public sources used by SIPRI.

This book illustrates the usefulness of independent sources of data on arms transfers. Much of the arms trade is not made transparent by the UN Register since it is limited to the seven major categories finally agreed by the Panel. A substantial amount of potentially destabilizing armaments are not included in any of the seven categories. For example, the UN Register does not include ground-to-air missiles or aerial refuelling aircraft. Second, not every country has participated in the first year of the Register, with some major recipient states conspicuously absent. Third, the UN Register is designed only to catch *deliveries* of arms. SIPRI's register continues to report *deliveries and orders*.

In the SIPRI data collection, an effort is made to report the financial aspects of an arms transfer whenever this information is available. The UN Register does not include this type of data. Financial data were specifically excluded and deemed beyond the mandate of the UN resolution. It is not important to know the value or the financial arrangements to assess the impact of weapon transfers on violent conflicts or tensions. If, however, the economic effects or the relationship between disarmament and development are the focus of the analysis, the exclusive knowledge of the number of items of transfers of major weapon systems and the exporter and importer country is not useful. While monetary values do not necessarily indicate military capability, they are an indicator of intent; and money spent on arms exports and imports is a potential source of funds that could be redirected into priority areas of social and economic development.

Many thought that the UN Register would be strictly a political exercise, assuming that all of the arms trade was publicly known. It was often said that this 'was not an intelligence exercise'. The results of the first year show that this is not true, as some very significant deals and much more data on deliveries are available in the UN Register than in data published by SIPRI. The fact that the information is officially submitted by governments will allow SIPRI to produce a much wider range of information and reconstruct specific transfers based on the government information. In sum, the two approaches to transparency enhance, reinforce and complement each other.

In 1968 SIPRI initiated the registering of the arms trade. In a major publication, *The Arms Trade With the Third World*, SIPRI states as its objective 'to throw light on the subject but also to find out what measures, if any, could be taken to limit this part of the global arms race'.[19] Twenty-five years later the UN General Assembly recognized 'that an increased level of openness and transparency in the field of armaments would enhance confidence, promote stability, help States to exercise restraint, ease tensions and strengthen regional and international peace and security'.[20] This book is the first effort to evaluate and compare these two registers using data on arms exported and imported in the same year (1992). Not only is the utility of each approach confirmed but the lessons from the first year's experience point the way to the further development of the UN Register.[21]

[19] SIPRI (note 18), p. v.
[20] UN General Assembly Resolution 46/36 L, 9 Dec. 1991, appendix A in *Report on the Register of Conventional Arms, Report of the Secretary-General* (note 15); see also annexe 3.
[21] The authors of this volume gratefully acknowledge the helpful comments received from Paul Claesson, Gerd Hagmeyer-Gaverus and Elisabeth Sköns, members of the SIPRI Arms Production and Arms Transfers Project, as well as their meticulous work on the SIPRI arms trade registers, without which this report could not have been written.

3. The first year of reporting

I. Government submissions

Compliance and non-compliance with the UN Register

All the United Nations member states and two observer states were invited by the UN Secretary-General to submit reports to the UN Register on a standardized form, consisting of data on their exports and imports of conventional arms. In addition, governments were asked to submit background information on military holdings, procurement through national production and relevant policies in any form they chose. Information on arms transfers was requested in seven weapon categories: battle tanks, armoured combat vehicles (ACVs), large-calibre artillery (LCA) systems, combat aircraft, attack helicopters, warships, and missiles and missile launchers.[1]

Table 3.1, prepared by the UN Office for Disarmament Affairs (ODA), summarizes the results of the first year of reporting. Seventy-eight governments, or over 40 per cent of those invited, complied with the UN General Assembly resolution and the request of the Secretary-General. Thirty-seven governments submitted forms with data on their arms imports and 24 on their arms exports. Thirty governments stated that they did not have any imports to report, and 41 did not have any export of weapons for 1992 in the seven categories to report during 1993.

Thirty countries gave explanations in a *note verbale* (some of them in addition to the standardized form on which they had reported). Background information was submitted by 34 of the 78 countries which reported. Such background information—which governments were asked to volunteer—varied widely in the details submitted. Several countries submitted data on military holdings and procurement through national production in the UN Register weapon categories. Other member states submitted excerpts from defence White Papers or White Books, while others submitted letters or notes explaining

[1] For a detailed description of the information requested and the standardized forms, see *Report on the Register of Conventional Arms, Report of the Secretary-General*, UN General Assembly document A/47/372, 14 Aug. 1992, reproduced in annexe 3.

their procedures and national regulations for imports or exports of weapons. In addition, the ODA, which is to maintain the information in a data base, received information that did not conform to the exact format of the UN Register.

Among the countries which submitted notes or remarks attached to their export form to explain their submissions, those of Australia, Germany and Russia were particularly interesting. In the German report, which was very detailed, it was stated, possibly as a reaction to domestic criticism on increasing German exports:

It becomes obvious from the figures that transfers mainly took place within NATO and to neighbouring Scandinavia. Deliveries to other countries were rather rare. This reflects the German arms export policy. Recent increases in exports are due to transfers of equipment of the former GDR armed forces mainly to other states parties to the CFE Treaty. This increase is temporary and does not indicate any change in the restrictive export policies pursued by the Federal Government.

Russian arms exports and export policy have led to much speculation in the media. The Russian Government's report to the UN on the export form clarifies some of the arms deals that had led to speculations. Russia informed the UN in three remarks that (a) 'sales to Syria of arms produced in the USSR and not supplied from the territory of the Russian Federation are not included'—these Syrian imports of weapons from the former Soviet Union apparently came from non-Russian sources; (b) 'transfers of arms to Azerbaijan, Georgia, Moldova and Belarus are not included' since these transfers are affected by the agreed division of the weapons of the former Soviet forces—a reference is made to the 1990 Treaty on Conventional Armed Forces in Europe (CFE Treaty) where ceilings on holdings have been agreed for the successor republics of the USSR; and (c) 'ground-to-ground missiles have not been supplied from Russia'.

In addition, the Australian return contained detailed explanations of Australia's arms transfers to make the report transparent.

Participation and non-participation

Although nearly 60 per cent of the UN member state governments did not report and others did not have any arms transfer data to report, this does not mean that the majority of arms exports and imports in

Table 3.1. Government submissions to the UN Register for 1992[a]

State	Data on imports	Data on exports	Explanation in *note verbale*	Background information
Argentina	nil	yes	..	no
Australia	yes	nil	..	yes
Austria	..	yes	..	yes
Belarus	nil	yes	..	no
Belgium	yes	nil	yes	yes
Bolivia	yes	nil	..	no
Brazil	yes	yes	..	yes
Bulgaria	yes	yes	..	yes
Canada	yes	yes	..	yes
Chile	yes	nil	..	yes
China	yes	yes	..	no
Colombia	yes	nil	yes	yes
Croatia	nil	nil	yes	no
Cuba	nil	nil	yes	no
Czech Republic	nil	yes	..	yes
Denmark	yes	nil	..	yes
Egypt	yes	yes	..	no
Fiji	nil	nil	..	no
Finland	yes	yes	..	yes
France	nil	yes	..	no
Georgia	nil	nil	yes	no
Germany	yes	yes	..	yes
Greece	yes	yes	yes	yes
Grenada	nil	blank form	..	no
Hungary	nil	nil	..	yes
Iceland	nil	nil	yes	no
India	yes	yes	..	no
Ireland	nil	nil	..	no
Israel	yes	yes	..	yes
Italy	yes	yes	..	yes
Japan	yes	nil	..	yes
Kazakhstan	nil	nil	yes	no
Lesotho	nil	nil	yes	no
Libya	nil	nil	yes	no
Liechtenstein	nil	nil	yes	no
Lithuania	yes	..	..	yes
Luxembourg	nil	nil	..	no
Malaysia	nil	nil	yes	no
Maldives	nil	nil	..	no
Malta	yes	nil	..	no
Mexico	..	..	yes	no

State	Data on imports	Data on exports	Explanation in *note verbale*	Background information
Mongolia	nil	nil	yes	no
Namibia	nil	nil	..	no
Nepal	yes	..	..	no
Netherlands	yes	yes	yes	yes
New Zealand	yes	nil	..	yes
Nicaragua	..	..	..	yes
Niger	see *note verbale*	nil	yes	no
Nigeria	..	..	yes	no
Norway	yes	blank form	..	yes
Oman	..	..	yes	no
Pakistan	yes	nil	..	no
Panama	..	..	yes	yes
Papua New Guinea	nil	nil	..	no
Paraguay	..	..	yes	no
Peru	yes	blank form	..	no
Philippines	yes	nil	yes	no
Poland	yes	yes	..	yes
Portugal	yes	nil	..	yes
Qatar	..	..	..	yes
South Korea	yes	nil	..	yes
Romania	yes	yes	..	no
Russia	nil	yes	..	no
Senegal	nil	nil	yes	no
Singapore	yes	nil	..	no
Slovak Republic	nil	yes	yes	no
Slovenia	nil	nil	yes	no
Solomon Islands	nil	nil	yes	no
South Africa	..	..	yes	no
Spain	yes	nil	..	yes
Sweden	yes	yes	..	yes
Switzerland	nil	nil	..	yes
Tunisia	..	..	yes	no
Turkey	yes	nil	..	yes
UK	yes	yes	..	yes
USA	yes	yes	yes	yes
Vanuatu	nil	nil	yes	no
Yugoslavia	nil	nil	yes	yes

a 'Yes' denotes submission of data on imports and/or exports. For uniform tabulation, 'nil' and 'no' are given as 'nil' reports. An ellipse (. .) in the imports or exports column indicates that no information was supplied. In some cases, however, an explanation was provided in the note of the country in question.

the seven UN categories were not recorded in the Register. Quite the opposite is the case. A first step towards demonstrating this fact is to compare the list of leading arms exporters and importers of conventional arms in 1992, ascertained from public sources, with a similar list drawn from those states which reported to the Register. This approach produces a rough estimate of the percentage of the trade made transparent in the Register.

Exporters

Table 3.2 lists the 19 leading arms-exporting countries, according to SIPRI data on 1992 deliveries, along with the value of these exports.[2] As can be seen, all but North Korea have reported to the UN Register. South Africa stated that, being under a UN embargo, it could not report any arms exports. Since North Korea's and South Africa's combined share (using SIPRI's valuation system) accounts for only 2 per cent of the exports, this methodology would indicate that 98 per cent of the publicly known arms exports in 1992 should be recorded in the Register. However, this percentage is uncertain, given the differences between the approach of SIPRI and that taken in the UN Register (see chapter 4). Furthermore, since no value for arms exports is recorded in the UN Register, it is not possible to give an exact amount or percentage of the exports that were reported. However, it is clear that, with all but North Korea and South Africa reporting, almost all of the arms exports have most likely been captured by the Register. Additionally, as shown in table 3.2, nine countries *not* listed by SIPRI as exporters of weapons in the UN Register categories in 1992 submitted export data for that year to the Register.

It should be noted that a few countries listed as exporters by SIPRI submitted nil reports or blank forms (Norway, Switzerland and Yugoslavia), stating in their returns that they did not export any weapons in the UN Register categories. The discrepancies between data in the UN and SIPRI registers are explained in detail in chapter 4. They are mainly due to the use of different definitions and the difficulties in determining exact delivery dates.

---

[2] For the list of leading exporters and importers of major conventional weapons and the definitions and methodologies applied, see *SIPRI Yearbook 1993: World Armaments and Disarmament* (Oxford University Press: Oxford, 1993), chapter 10.

Table 3.2. The leading exporters of major conventional weapons in 1992[a]
Figures are in 1990 US$ m.

Country	SIPRI value[b]	Exports reported to the UN Register
1. USA	8 429	yes
2. Russia	2 043	yes
3. Germany	1 928	yes
4. China	1 535	yes
5. France	1 151	yes
6. UK	952	yes
7. Czechoslovakia[c]	779	yes
8. Italy	335	yes
9. North Korea	313	no
10. Netherlands	305	yes
11. Sweden	113	yes
12. Switzerland	83	nil
13. Brazil	36	yes
14. Poland	35	yes
15. South Africa[d]	23	no
16. Yugoslavia	21	nil
17. Canada	17	yes
18. Norway	17	blank form
19. Greece	8	yes
Countries with no recorded exports for 1992 in SIPRI data		
Austria	–	yes
Belarus	–	yes
Bulgaria	–	yes
Egypt	–	yes
Finland	–	yes
India	–	yes
Israel	–	yes
Nicaragua	–	yes
Romania	–	yes

[a] The table lists all countries that, according to information available to SIPRI, exported weapons in the UN Register categories.

[b] According to the SIPRI valuation system. For the methodology applied, see *SIPRI Yearbook 1993: World Armaments and Disarmament* (Oxford University Press: Oxford, 1993), appendix 10D, pp. 519–20.

[c] Includes both the Czech and the Slovak Republics, which reported separately to the UN. (Czechoslovakia split into two independent states on 1 Jan. 1993.)

[d] South Africa stated that it could not report arms exports since it was under a UN embargo.

Source: For col. 2, SIPRI data base; col. 3, UN Register.

Further evidence that the UN Register includes nearly all the 1992 arms deliveries is provided by information from a US Congressional Research Service report.[3] Using US Government data, the report lists the eight leading suppliers, all of which have reported to the UN Register: Belgium, Brazil, China, France, Germany, Russia, the UK and the USA.

Importers

The reporting record of major arms importers is not as positive, as shown in table 3.3. All the 15 leading importers of the industrialized world which imported weapons in the UN Register categories in 1992 reported to the UN. Only Argentina, Chile, China, Egypt, India, Israel, South Korea and Pakistan among the group of the 15 leading importers in the developing world reported; 7 of these 15 importers did not report.

The arms imports reported represent approximately 65 per cent of the SIPRI value of the trade in major conventional weapons in 1992, according to the SIPRI valuation system.

The lower level of reporting by importers is confirmed by the data of the Congressional Research Service report quoted above. Of the 10 leading recipients of conventional weapons in the developing world, only China, Egypt, India and Israel reported their imports to the United Nations, while Saudi Arabia, Syria, the United Arab Emirates, Kuwait and Iran (as well as Taiwan)[4] did not report.

Information on imports through export reports

Although the reporting record of some of the major arms-importing countries is disappointing, information on arms deliveries to the major importing countries and certain regions can at least partly be inferred from export returns, since the final importer is always given in the report.

To illustrate this fact an import return was constructed by the authors for Saudi Arabia—a large importer that did not report—on the

---

[3] Grimmett, R. F., *Conventional Arms Transfers to the Third World, 1985–1992*, CRS *Report for Congress* (US Library of Congress, Congressional Research Service: Washington, DC, 19 July 1993).

[4] Taiwan, a major arms importer, is not a UN member state and was thus not asked to report.

Table 3.3. The leading importers of major conventional weapons in 1992
Figures are in 1990 US$ m.

Country	SIPRI value[a]	Imports reported to the UN Register
Industrialized world		
1. Greece	1 918	yes
2. Turkey	1 511	yes
3. Japan	1 095	yes
4. UK	1 051	yes
5. USA	726	yes
6. Finland	413	yes
7. Australia	398	yes
8. Spain	370	yes
9. Canada	234	yes
10. Norway	183	yes
11. Netherlands	181	yes
12. Germany	144	yes
13. Italy	110	yes
14. Belgium	86	yes
15. Denmark	59	yes
Developing world		
1. India	1 197	yes
2. Saudi Arabia	883	no
3. Iran	877	no
4. Thailand	869	no
5. Syria	716	no
6. Israel	709	yes
7. Egypt	621	yes
8. China	609	yes
9. Pakistan	432	yes
10. South Korea	414	yes
11. Taiwan	285	no (not a UN member state)
12. Bangladesh	224	no
13. Chile	204	yes
14. Kuwait	190	no
15. Argentina	139	nil

[a] According to the SIPRI valuation system. The figures include the value of all deliveries and licensed production in 1992 of all weapon types, including those not in the UN Register weapon categories. For the SIPRI valuation methodology applied, see *SIPRI Yearbook 1993: World Armaments and Disarmament* (Oxford University Press: Oxford, 1993), appendix 10D, pp. 519–20.

Source: For col. 2, SIPRI data base; col. 3, UN Register.

APPENDIX B (concluded)
Standardized forms for reporting international transfers of conventional arms

IMPORTS
Report of international conventional arms transfers
(according to United Nations General Assembly resolution 46/36 L)
Reporting country: Saudi Arabia
Calendar year: 1992

A	B	C	D*	E*	REMARKS**	
Category (I–VII)	Final exporter State(s)	Number of items	State of origin (if not exporter)	Intermediate location (if any)	Description of item	Comments on the transfer
I. Battle tanks	1) 2) 3)					
II. Armoured combat vehicles	1) Canada 2) UK 3) USA	262 29 192			Wheeled armoured personnel carrier	
III. Large calibre artillery systems	1) France 2) 3)	175				
IV. Combat aircraft	1) UK 2) USA 3)	1 10				
V. Attack helicopters	1) 2) 3)					
VI. Warships	1) 2) 3)					
VII. Missiles and missile launchers	1) Brazil 2) France 3) UK	50 328 6 48			SS30, SS40, SS60 rockets for ASTROS II	

Background information provided: yes/no

*   See para. 18 of the present report.
** See para. 19 of the present report.

Figure 3.1. Constructed arms imports return for Saudi Arabia, 1992: based on supplier countries' export returns

basis of the returns of its major suppliers: the USA, the UK, Canada, France and Brazil (see figure 3.1). According to publicly available information, there was no other supplier of conventional weapons to Saudi Arabia in the UN Register categories in 1992. Thus the constructed report for Saudi Arabia can be taken as a realistic picture of Saudi Arabia's imports. Note the variation in detail for each entry, as not every supplier chose to submit data in the 'description of item' and 'comments' columns of the Register form. A similar return could be produced for numerous other countries (Bangladesh, Indonesia and many others) that imported weapons from countries which reported arms exports. This exercise is not possible for countries that imported weapons from North Korea or South Africa, however, since they did not submit a return or export data for 1992.

II. Verification by cross-checking: a unique feature of the UN Register

Verification procedures and the UN Register

The UN Register, as a confidence-building measure designed to promote transparency, is very different from arms control arrangements based on a treaty. The word 'verification' does not exist in the UN resolution or any implementing documents.

Despite the absence of formal verification procedures in the Register, the demand for verification of data will not disappear. In its recent study on verification, the United Nations named five important functions that will be performed one way or another in any agreement or measure designed to guide or control the behaviour of states. These include assessing implementation, generating confidence, dealing with uncertainties, discouraging non-compliance and providing for timely warning.[5] All these functions are valid and relevant for the Register. The difference is that no formal mechanisms such as on-site inspection, 'open skies' air reconnaissance, verification by national technical means, the establishment of a neutral and multilateral inspection team, or any other such method will be used to verify the reliability and accuracy of the data. Additionally, the role of the UN Secretariat will be minimal when it comes to verification: 'The Panel of Governmental Technical Experts made it clear that the task of the UN Secretariat is to file and distribute the incoming reports from member states but not to check or verify them'.[6]

In the future such mechanisms may be developed. However, for the first two years (the returns for arms transfers in 1992 and 1993), the Register must rely on several informal approaches which are more appropriate for a confidence-building measure. The first of these is the comparison of Register entries with publicly known data. Chapter 4 engages in this type of verification technique since it compares the UN Register data with the data from public sources published in the SIPRI arms register. The second technique is self-contained within the Register itself. Member states are requested to report both exports and imports, setting up a situation where an exporting state

[5] United Nations Department [now Office] for Disarmament Affairs, *The Role of the United Nations in the Field of Verification* (UN: New York, 1991).

[6] Wulf, H., 'The United Nations Register of Conventional Arms', *SIPRI Yearbook 1993* (note 2), appendix 10F (see annexe 3 for an excerpt from this appendix).

may report a transfer of, say, 40 tanks but the importer of these tanks may or may not report them. As seen in the results of the first year, not only did both of these situations occur, but in some cases the exporter and importer reported different numbers for the same transfer. However, the data submitted will be made public each year in a report by the Secretary-General, thereby giving any member state, and the public at large, the opportunity to 'analyse the national submissions to the Register, compare them with other public or national intelligence data, and identify apparent inconsistencies and inaccuracies'.[7] The Register procedures developed to this point do not provide for any specific ways for states to raise questions on the data, but traditional bilateral and multilateral diplomacy was most frequently mentioned when the question arose in various deliberations.

Despite the absence of a formal verification mechanism, the cross-checking feature of the Register has the potential to accomplish the five functions of verification outlined in the aforementioned UN study.

Cross-checking the data from the first year

Methodology

As seen in annexe 1, the government submissions to the UN Register contain both exports and imports of weapons. In assessing the effectiveness of the Register, the first step is to develop a list of *discrete arms transfers* by eliminating the duplicate entries which occur when both the arms exporter and importer report the same transfer. The following procedure was used. First, each entry on the *export forms* was recorded as an arms transfer (a total of 159). Then all of the entries made using the *import forms* were examined, entering as arms transfers only those which did *not* appear on the export forms (an additional 33). Three types of entry were involved, as shown below.

Exporter country	Category	Importer	No. of items	Description
Argentina	Combat aircraft	Sri Lanka	4	IA-58 Pucara

---

[7] Chalmers, M. and Greene, O., *Implementing and Developing the United Nations Register of Conventional Arms* (Department of Peace Studies, University of Bradford: May 1993), p. 46 (see annexe 3 for an excerpt from this report).

The above entry from the export form of Argentina is recorded as an arms transfer. It is most likely one deal for four aircraft.

In other entries, it is not as clear that the entry is in fact one deal. In the example below, the artillery pieces could be of different types or could have been transferred in several discrete packages. However, for the purposes of this analysis, it is listed as one transfer.

Exporter country	Category	Importer	No. of items	Description
France	Large-calibre artillery	Saudi Arabia	175	None given

When examining the import forms, those transfers already entered in the export forms are eliminated from the master list, as shown in the examples below.

Importer country	Category	Exporter	No. of items	Status
Bolivia	Large-calibre artillery	China	36	Not reported as an export by China and *is* therefore recorded as an arms transfer
Brazil	Large-calibre artillery	UK	4	Reported by the UK as an export and is a duplicate entry; therefore it is *not* added as an arms transfer

Using this approach to tabulating a list of arms transfers in the UN Register for 1992, there were a total of 192 discrete arms transfers; 159, or 83 per cent, of these entries came from the export forms, with the remaining 33 from the import forms. Figure 3.2 breaks down these entries by UN Register weapon category.

A second way of viewing the data is by number of items. The number of items per arms transfer varies widely, from one tank to the 50 328 ASTROS rockets delivered to Saudi Arabia by Brazil. In table 3.4 the data are shown disaggregated by number of items per category.

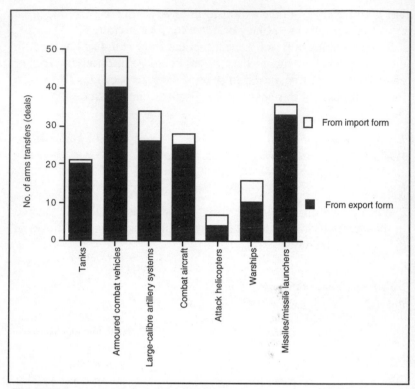

Figure 3.2. Arms transfers recorded in the UN Register for 1992
Note: Data 'from import form' are those arms transfers which are not recorded on export forms.

Table 3.4. Items recorded in the UN Register for 1992, by weapon type

Category	No. of items, UN Register[a]
Tanks	1 733
Armoured combat vehicles	1 625
Large-calibre artillery systems	1 676
Combat aircraft	270
Attack helicopters	40
Warships	33
Missiles and missile launchers	67 838

[a] In 16 cases, exporters and importers reported the same transfer but with different numbers. In this and other tables in this chapter, the number of discrete entries is used.

Table 3.5. Total number of weapons imported in 1992, by region of recipient country

Figures are for numbers of weapon systems transferred.

Region	Tanks	ACVs	LCA	Combat aircraft	Heli-copters	War-ships	Missiles/launchers
Asia	117	40	146	59	–	4	304
Near East[a]	165	755	510	96	–	1	52 379
Sub-Saharan Africa	25	8	74	5	–	–	–
Europe[b]	109	192	547	9	–	13	13
NATO Europe	1 295	573	340	83	16	13	14 812
Latin America	14	16	58	18	23	1	18
North America	8	41	1	–	1	1	312
Total	**1 733**	**1 625**	**1 676**	**270**	**40**	**33**	**67 838**

[a] The Near East includes the Middle East, North Africa and the Persian Gulf states.
[b] Europe includes the CIS and East European states.

The regional distribution of these items is shown in table 3.5. As this table indicates, a significant percentage of the arms delivered in 1992 was to NATO countries, owing to the redistribution of weapons, or 'cascading', resulting from the CFE Treaty. The Near East also continued to be a major recipient region. It should be noted that the missiles total of 67 838 is skewed by the delivery of 50 328 ASTROS rockets to Saudi Arabia by Brazil and 13 350 RP/C M-26 and M-28 rockets by Germany.

Table 3.6. The leading exporters of major weapon systems in 1992

Figures are for numbers of weapon systems transferred.

Country	Tanks	ACVs	LCA	Combat aircraft	Heli-copters	War-ships	Missiles/launchers
China	97	2	215	–	–	2	24
France	–	36	215	16	1	–	26
Germany	140	136	449	18	1	19	13 540
Russia	7	213	–	31	3	7	144
UK	31	46	13	19	–	1	446
USA	1 255	719	167	165	6	1	2 891
Total[a]	**1 733**	**1 625**	**1 676**	**270**	**40**	**33**	**67 838**

[a] Including all other exporters.

Table 3.6 disaggregates the 192 arms transfers by exporter and weapon type, making it clear that the USA was the dominant arms supplier in 1992. Germany was the second largest supplier, with weapons exported in each of the seven weapon categories. The USA led in the exports of land combat systems and exported 61 per cent of all combat aircraft, and Germany led the major exporters in large-calibre artillery systems.

As for individual importer states, table 3.7 shows that Greece and Turkey were the recipients which benefited from the 'cascading' transfers resulting from the CFE Treaty.

Table 3.7. The leading importers of major weapon systems in 1992

Figures are for numbers of weapon systems imported.

Country	Tanks	ACVs	LCA	Combat aircraft	Heli-copters	War-ships	Missiles/ launchers
Finland	97	88	447	–	–	1	5
Greece	592	206	243	33	–	13	128
Saudi Arabia	–	483	175	11	–	–	50 382
Turkey	588	325	75	46	6	–	1 164
UK	1	10	18	–	–	–	7 778
Total[a]	1 733	1 625	1 676	270	40	33	67 838

[a] Including all other importers.

Results

At least eight different types of result were exhibited in the 1992 reporting.

1. *Matching items.* An entry is made as either an export or an import, and the state at the other end of the deal has reported similar data. The highest level of verification occurs when both parties employ maximum transparency to report the transfer. For example, Italy reported exporting six MB-339C combat aircraft to New Zealand, and New Zealand reported importing the same six aircraft. Many of the 'confirmed' cases at this level of transparency involved NATO states reporting widely known transfers related to the 1990 CFE Treaty and the 1992 CFE-1A Agreement. For example, the Netherlands and Greece produced similar information in reporting the

transfer of 171 M-30 4.2-inch mortars. Both gave the model number, and the Netherlands referred in the 'Comments' column to 'CFE cascading' while Greece gave a more detailed 25-word comment. This example also points out that, even in the case of 'confirmed' cases, there was very little evidence that partners in a transfer had co-ordinated their returns to the point of settling on common language.

In a few cases states involved in a transfer reported similar but not identical numbers of items. For example, France reported exporting 26 large-calibre artillery systems to Singapore, while Singapore reported importing 24. For the purposes of this analysis, if the data obviously refer to the same deal and the number of items listed by both parties is exactly the same or within 15 per cent, this is a matched item case. These cases are labelled as *'confirmed'* in the aggregate data analysis below in this section.

2. *Differences.* An entry is made as either an export or an import, and the state at the other end of the deal reported data which appear to be similar but the number of items reported differs significantly. For example, the United States reported sending 492 tanks to Greece while Greece reported importing only 347 of these tanks. There were 16 such cases of 192 arms transfers, all but one involving the USA as the exporting state. In the data analysis these cases are labelled as *'different number'*.

An analysis of these cases generates at least one hypothesis for the difference in items reported. When the transfer involved the CFE Treaty 'cascade' process, there was agreement on numbers. Both the USA and Greece, for example, reported 72 M-110-A2 howitzers, but in other non-CFE Treaty cascade deals between the USA and Greece, involving tanks, missiles and warships, either the numbers were different or the deal was not reported. In all but one of these cases, the NATO recipient reported fewer items than the USA. In another example, both the USA and Japan reported an arms transfer under missiles and missile launchers: the US number of items exported to Japan was 109 and the Japanese number imported was 76. Given the close relationship between these two states and their commitment to the Register, procedural differences as the cause of the discrepancies would appear to be the most likely hypothesis.

3. *Non-participation.* An entry is made as either an export or import, and the state at the other end of the deal has not participated in the Register by submitting data. Therefore, this entry cannot be con-

firmed by cross-checking. Some key transfers fall into this category. The largest was the Brazilian export to Saudi Arabia of 50 328 rockets of several types for the previously exported ASTROS II multiple rocket launcher (MRL) system. Others include Bulgaria sending 210 large-calibre artillery pieces to Syria, and China exporting 106 large-calibre artillery pieces to Iran. It should be noted that in only 18 entries (31 per cent of the total non-participation cases) did the reporting state use the Remarks columns on the form to describe the model or type of item transferred, a further diminution of the transparency of the data. In the data analysis these cases are labelled 'NP', for non-participation by one of the partners in the transfer.

Of 51 arms transfers classified as non-participating, 23 (45 per cent) arose from the non-participation of states in the Near East region, which points to the critical importance of participation by these states. Only when Saudi Arabia and other states in that region report will the accumulation of conventional weapons be confirmed and transparent and allow for the effective development of the confidence building and early warning for which the Register was designed.

4. *Non-reporting.* An entry is made either as an export or import, and the state at the other end of the deal, although participating in the Register by submitting data, did not report this particular deal or entry. This entry also cannot be confirmed by cross-checking. These discrepancies are more intriguing, since the presumption is that the state not reporting this particular deal has made a major foreign policy decision by participating in the Register. Sixty-seven entries (35 per cent) fall in this non-reporting category and among them are some major transfers. Among these are five deals involving the same missile in its operational or test version—the RP/C M-26/28 rocket for the multiple-launch rocket system (MLRS)—reported by Germany as an export to the United Kingdom, France and Italy. The total number of unreported missiles in these five deals is 6462. None of these recipients reported the transfer, suggesting that there is a procedural misunderstanding, perhaps related to the co-production aspects of this MLRS. It provides further proof that there was minimal co-ordination among arms transfer partners, even in the highly integrated NATO environment, and enhances the hypothesis that partners to a transfer can disagree on definitional grounds. Cases in this category are labelled 'NR', for non-reporting, in the data analysis.

This 'procedural' hypothesis may also explain the rather high number of NR cases for ships, where 76 per cent of all warships registered were not reported, in some cases by the exporter and in others by the importer. Germany has made public its sale of a submarine to South Korea, yet South Korea, whose Register submission includes designations, does not mention importing this submarine. Definitional problems are also at work in the case of ship imports by Greece, which reported receiving four corvettes from Germany as aid and the lease of seven frigates from the USA. In the case of Malta declaring the import of three patrol boats from Italy and four patrol boats from Germany (equipment from the former German Democratic Republic), it appears to be a case of over-reporting and erring on the side of transparency, since it is highly unlikely that these ships would carry missiles and qualify for the Register category.

A significant number of the NR cases (13 of 74, or 18 per cent) involve German exports not reported by the recipient. It became clear in various international forums that Germany was very keen not only to establish the Register but also to complete the submission of data with maximum transparency. It may be the case that as a policy choice Germany decided to err on the side of transparency.[8]

5. *Differences in transparency.* The exporter or importer may provide full details of the transfer, to include model, type and description, while the state at the other end of the deal does not. Such detailed information can lead to adding significant transparency and reliability to the data. For example, the UK reported importing 6888 missiles and missile launchers from Germany. This could represent a large number of combinations of types of missiles and launchers, but when examining the German export data, it can be seen that they reported exporting 6888 RP/C M-26 rockets for the MLRS. Since Germany was the only major arms supplier to use the Remarks columns of the report, a significant percentage of the transparency can be attributed to Germany. Other exporter states whose returns were particularly transparent include Canada, Italy and the Netherlands.

One of the categories made most transparent in terms of numbers of items was that of missiles and missile launchers. It is arguably the least defined category and, with such a wide variety of types and models, states reporting simply the number of items would add little

[8] Different cases of non-reporting are discussed in the next chapter, where the SIPRI register is compared with the UN Register.

to the actual knowledge of missiles transferred. However, thanks to Brazil's transparency in giving the exact model and type of the rockets it transferred to Saudia Arabia (SS-30/40/60 rockets for the ASTROS II MRL system), a significant percentage of the items in the missile and missile launcher category were transparent. As mentioned above, Germany's submission also contributed to a high level of transparency in these data.

6. *Limited transparency*. The exporter or importer state may provide minimal details on the entry (e.g., 38 tanks) and the state at the other end of the deal either does not participate in the Register or does not report that particular transfer. In this case the cross-check confirms the minimum level of transparency for that transfer. There were many examples of this phenomenon, especially where a major supplier which did not supply information in the Remarks columns (the USA, France and the UK) exported to states which imported many items but either did not participate in the Register (e.g., Saudi Arabia and other Persian Gulf states) or did not choose to provide model or type information in the Remarks columns.

7. *Differences in aggregation*. In a similar case, the exporter or importer state may provide minimal details on the entry (e.g., 38 tanks) and the state at the other end of the deal breaks the transfer into two component parts and provides details (e.g., 20 Type A1 tanks and 18 Type A3 tanks). This led to some confusion in aggregating the data for this analysis and, to be consistent, in cases like this the split deal was aggregated into one entry and classified as confirmed. In an actual case, the United States reported an export of 88 missiles and missile launchers to Canada, which reported an import of 75 Sea Sparrow ship-launched surface-to-air missiles and 5 Harpoon ship-launched surface-to-surface missiles, a total of 80. For the purpose of the analysis, this is recorded as one arms transfer of 80–88 missiles and categorized as matching items or confirmed.[9]

8. *Non-UN Register equipment*. In a final situation, some states entered data which clearly did not fall within the definitions of the categories of the Register (e.g., Malta reported the import of small patrol craft not armed with missiles). In this case the entries were retained in the data for the purpose of this report.

---

[9] It should be noted that in taking into account the cases occurring in this category (6), the number of arms transfers increases to 198.

Level of verification of data using the cross-checking system

The following tables disaggregate the data according to result categories 1–4 described in the previous section.

Table 3.8 reveals that 27 per cent of the arms transfer deals can be considered 'confirmed' by the definitions explained above. If the Register is to be used as an early warning of weapon accumulations, a more appropriate unit of analysis is the item. When the data are analysed at this level, it can be seen that only 12 per cent of the items can be confirmed or verified by both exporter and importer reporting similar information on specific transfers. Sixty-eight per cent of the transfers cannot be confirmed since one of the partners in the transfer either did not participate (NP) or did not report (NR) the transfer. Several caveats are in order.

The very large transfer of 50 328 ASTROS rockets by Brazil to Saudi Arabia significantly skews the data. For example, had Saudi

Table 3.8. Results of cross-checking exporter and importer returns for 1992

Category	No./% confirmed	No./% diff.	No./% NR	No./% NP
Transfers N = 192	51 (27%)	17 (9%)[a]	73 (38%)	51 (27%)
Items N = 73 215	8 935 (12%)	2 985 (4%)	7 527 (10%)	53 768 (74%)

Transfers	Number of deals reported
Items	Number of weapon systems reported
Confirmed	The data entered were reported by both exporter and importer
Diff.	The data entered were reported by both exporter and importer, but the numbers differ in their returns
NR	Non-reporting; the other state in the transaction (exporter or importer) participated in the Register but did not report this particular transfer
NP	Non-participation; the other state in the transaction (exporter or importer) did not participate in or submit any data to the Register

[a] In the 17 cases there is a difference in the number of items reported by the exporter and importer state. In most cases the figures submitted by the exporter state are higher.

Table 3.9. Level of verification, by weapon type

Category	No./% confirmed	No./% diff.	No./% NR	No./% NP
Tanks N = 1 733	329 (19%)	1 241 (66%)	63 (4%)	100 (6%)
ACVs N = 1 625	292 (18%)	225 (14%)	247 (15%)	861 (53%)
LCA N = 1 676	799 (48%)	–	147 (9%)	725 (43%)
Cbt Acft N = 270	122 (45%)	60 (22%)	35 (13%)	53 (20%)
Atk Helo N = 40	17 (43%)	–	23 (57%)	–
Warships N = 33	4 (12%)	1 (3%)	25 (76%)	3 (9%)
M/Ml N = 67 838	7 392 (11%)	1 462 (2%)	6 962 (10%)	52 022 (77%)
M/Ml N (minus all reported ASTROS and RP/C M rockets) = 3 776	504 (13%)	1 462 (39%)	136 (4%)	1 694 (45%)

Confirmed	The data entered were reported by both exporter and importer
Diff.	The data entered were reported by both exporter and importer, but the numbers differ in their returns
NR	Non-reporting; the other state in the transaction (exporter or importer) participated in the Register but did not report this particular transfer
NP	Non-participation; the other state in the transaction (exporter or importer) did not participate in or submit any data to the Register

Arabia reported the import of these rockets, the percentage of 'confirmed' items would increase to roughly 80 per cent of the items reported to the Register. If this deal is treated as an outlier and eliminated from the analysis, the number of items in the NP category drops to 3436 and the percentage of items confirmed increases to 39 per cent. If the items in which the exporters and importers disagreed only on the number of items in the deal are treated as 'confirmed' items, the percentage of confirmed items increases to 52 per cent.

In table 3.9, the data are arrayed by category of equipment. In four of the categories (tanks, large-calibre artillery, combat aircraft, and missiles and missile launchers) exporters and importers reported different numbers of items on one or more transfer.

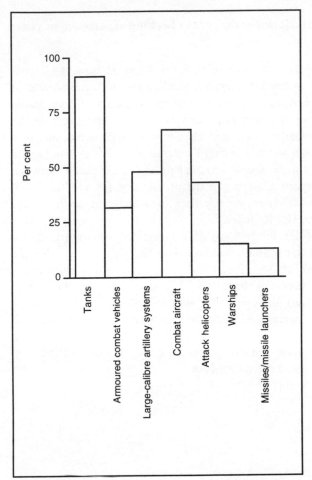

Figure 3.3. Verified arms transfers, by weapon type

In figure 3.3 it can more clearly be seen that there is a major difference in the level of verified or confirmed data when disaggregating by
weapon category. In the case of tanks, when the percentages for
'confirmed' and 'different number' are aggregated, 90 per cent of all
tank transfers reported were verified. Only 13 per cent of the missiles
and missile launchers were verified, increasing to 52 per cent when
excluding the large Brazilian rocket delivery to Saudi Arabia. Particularly noteworthy is the warship category, where only four ship transfers could be verified using the cross-checking system.

Summary and conclusions: the cross-checking experience in year one

The above analysis is a very brief assessment of how the cross-checking system of the UN Register worked during the first year of reporting. It is clear that a great deal of transparency and verifiable data can be generated using the cross-checking approach of the Register. In this analysis the cross-checking is unobtrusive, that is, a manipulation of the submitted data by the analyst. What is unknown is exactly how much actual cross-checking took place between exporters and importers as part of the preparation for submission of data at the national level or whether they may do so in future submissions to the UN Register.

In short, one of the real benefits of the Register—the motivation to submit valid and transparent data based on the presumption that the trading partner will do so—is not really captured in this assessment. The time period between the first and second reporting date, from 1 October 1993 until 30 April 1994, will provide the opportunity for analysts, member states and above all the expert group which will meet in 1994 to go beyond mere data analysis to ascertain and perhaps further develop the strength of the cross-checking verification tool embedded in the Register process.

4. A comparison of SIPRI data with the UN Register of Conventional Arms

I. Introduction

Since the publication of its first arms trade register in 1969, SIPRI has been the logical starting-point for those seeking information on individual arms deals. The activities of SIPRI have played a part in convincing a significant number of governments that arms transfers cannot be hidden entirely and that they have more to gain than to lose from public disclosure of elements of this trade. The SIPRI data base stores information on approximately 15 000 individual bilateral transfers of major conventional weapons for the period 1950–93. The information is collected from public sources; SIPRI has no independent or special access to information.

This chapter compares the data as reported in the 1993 returns to the UN Register made by governments for calendar year 1992 with data reported in the SIPRI arms trade register in the *SIPRI Yearbook 1993*.[1] The comparison in this chapter shows the same pattern as in chapter 3—some matching records but a large number of records which differ from or are unique to one of the registers. This chapter offers possible explanations for these differences.

A comparison of the two registers (see annexes 1 and 2) underlines that, while the UN Register is a short document containing only 192 discrete entries, the SIPRI register contains over 800 individual entries. This is in itself sufficient to indicate that there are important differences between the two registers.

Discrepancies could occur as a result of one of three possibilities. The two extremes are (*a*) that the information in the SIPRI data base is incorrect or (*b*) that information has been wrongly reported by governments in their returns to the UN Register. The third possibility is confusion stemming from the different structure, scope and methodologies underpinning the two registers. The analysis below indicates that there are examples of all three types of discrepancy. Although the

[1] See annexe 2 for a modified version of the SIPRI register as it appeared as appendix 10C in *SIPRI Yearbook 1993: World Armaments and Disarmament* (Oxford University Press: Oxford, 1993).

possibility of 'cheating' exists, there is no evidence that it has occurred since all the discrepancies discovered in comparing the two registers can be explained in other ways.

II. Structural differences in the registers

The registers overlap in their focus on narrow equipment categories. Both use country-to-country transfers as their organizing principle rather than focusing on the manufacturer (as the exporting actor) or the army, navy, air force, coast guard, para-military or internal security forces (as the importing actor). Nevertheless, there are three structural differences between the SIPRI and UN registers which make comparisons difficult and which make discrepancies between them inevitable.

1. The UN Register is confined to recording weapon deliveries, while the SIPRI register records all deals made or ongoing in a given calendar year. While SIPRI value statistics are derived only from delivered systems, the SIPRI register includes information on all orders, whether or not deliveries have taken place during the reported year. The SIPRI register also differentiates between individual deals made for the same category or type of weapon system to be delivered to one country, while the UN Register requires that governments state only the total number of items of one category supplied to one country; the UN does not require governments to split them up in specific deals or different weapon types within the category. For example, SIPRI reports the export of M-113-A2 and M-2 Bradley armoured combat vehicles (ACVs) from the USA to Saudi Arabia as two separate entries, while the US return to the UN Register gives only one entry informing that 192 unspecified ACVs have been delivered.

2. The UN Register is confined to the seven weapon categories defined in the 1992 UN *Report on the Register of Conventional Arms.* The six SIPRI weapon categories defined by the Institute are aircraft, armoured vehicles, artillery, guidance and radar systems, missiles and warships. Of the SIPRI weapon categories, one—artillery—is very similar to the category large-calibre artillery systems used in the UN Register. In the other categories there are significant differences (see section III for a comparison of the weapon categories in the two registers).

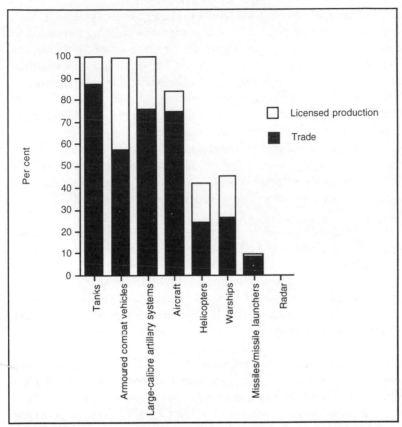

Figure 4.1. Percentage of items reported by SIPRI for 1992 which fit the UN Register definitions

Note: The SIPRI category 'guidance and radar systems' does not fit any of the UN Register categories.

3. The third structural difference between the two registers is that the UN Register is confined to direct deliveries of complete systems, while the SIPRI register also includes weapons produced under licence by the recipient country.

As illustrated in figure 4.1, licensed production of weapons falling within the UN Register definitions can be quite substantial, such as the case of ACVs, 42 per cent of which are, according to SIPRI, licence produced. However, in some cases the borderline is not very clear between actual licensed production and assembly of a kit, with nothing more than unpacking, some bolting and painting remaining to be done by the licensee. This means that in some cases SIPRI records a transfer as a direct delivery, while the importer and exporter may consider it as licensed production. The opposite may also be true, as in the case of Belgium and Italy reporting the transfer of 10 A-109 attack helicopters. According to the sources on which the SIPRI register is based, these helicopters are assembled in Belgium (with some degree of indigenous input), and reporting to the UN is therefore not mandatory. The guidelines for the UN Register do not solve this problem; the only solution would be to have a more comprehensive register which also incorporated procurement through national production.

The SIPRI value statistics are based on all imports or exports as given for a country in the SIPRI data base. In a few cases countries figuring high on the list of importers or exporters do so because they import or export weapons that do not fall within the seven UN Register categories or because of licensed production, which for the purpose of the UN Register is simply national production and therefore exempt from reporting. As can be seen from table 3.3 (chapter 3), India is reported as the leading importer among the developing countries. However, the Indian return to the UN does not include many items, nor do the returns from the exporters to India. The entry for India in the SIPRI register (annexe 2) shows that most of the trade is licensed production. In the SIPRI value tables,[2] a percentage of the value for items produced under licence is taken as trade between exporter and importer because in most cases the licenser will supply many parts of the weapon to the licensee. For example, the Type-1500 submarine built under a German licence in India does not need to be reported to the UN Register by India or Germany (although Germany did report delivery of a 'submarine kit'). In the SIPRI value tables this is reflected by taking 90 per cent of the trade value of the submarine as trade between Germany and India.

Taking all these factors into account, the above-mentioned major discrepancy in the number of reported entries (192 deals as against over 800) is changed drastically: SIPRI reports 418 separate deals of weapons falling within the seven UN Register categories, of which 78 are deliveries from or orders for licensed production and 197 are deals

[2] *SIPRI Yearbook 1993* (note 1), appendix 10B, pp. 476–82.

on order for which no deliveries were recorded for 1992, leaving 143 entries on deliveries of weapons comparable to the UN Register.

III. Comparing the SIPRI and UN registers

In comparing the SIPRI register with the UN Register the differences initially seem to be irreconcilable. Structural differences which make comparisons difficult are listed in section II above. Some instances reflect the fact that in the first years there will inevitably be some 'sand in the gears' when it comes to implementing the UN Register.

For comparative purposes there are five classes of record.

1. Records of items not falling under the UN Register categories but included in the SIPRI register.
2. Records which match—the two registers report deliveries of approximately the same number of items (± 10 per cent) of the same equipment type.
3. Records which partly match—there is enough common information to suggest that the same deal is being described but the number of items delivered differs by more than 10 per cent.
4. Records which appear in the UN Register but not in the SIPRI register.
5. Records which appear in the SIPRI register but not in the UN Register.

Class 1: records of items not falling in the UN Register categories

The scope of the SIPRI data base is wider than the UN Register categories, as shown in figure 4.1. The UN categories of tanks and large-calibre artillery systems are completely covered by the SIPRI data base. The armoured combat vehicle category is only slightly less comprehensive than the SIPRI data base. The only difference is that SIPRI records all armoured vehicles, without the UN limitations of gun calibre or troop-carrying capacity. However, the number of armoured vehicles that fall outside the scope of the UN Register is very limited (for 1992 only 0.6 per cent), as in the case of six Buffel armoured recovery vehicles (ARVs) imported by the Netherlands. For the other categories a comparison by pure numbers gives a distorted picture. SIPRI includes all aircraft and helicopters, whereas the UN

Register is confined to types fitted for combat roles, not for support roles. Of all the aircraft reported by SIPRI in 1992, 75 per cent fit the UN definition of a combat aircraft, while for helicopters only 42 per cent fit the UN attack helicopter category. For ships the picture is nearly the same: 45 per cent would be considered a warship under the UN Register category. The least comparable case is missiles and missile launchers: slightly less than 10 per cent of all missiles and launchers reported by SIPRI as delivered in 1992 would fall under the UN Register category. The rest either do not fit the range criterion of over 25 km, such as all anti-tank missiles, or are part of the exemption to the Register, surface-to-air missiles (SAMs). A last major difference between SIPRI and the UN are radar systems. SIPRI reports all surveillance, battlefield and fire control radars when they do not form an integrated part of a sold platform. The UN Register does not include radars at all.

Class 2: matching records

Perfect matches—with the records of the importing government, the exporting government and SIPRI agreeing on the number of items and year of delivery—are rare. This is partly because of the internal inconsistencies of the UN Register, as described in chapter 3.

An example of a perfect match is the delivery of four L119 artillery pieces to Brazil by the UK. Another is the delivery to Chile of 10 combat aircraft—the A-37 Dragonfly—by the United States.

Instances of a return by either the importer or the exporter, but not both, which matches a SIPRI record are more frequent. In these cases the differences can often be explained by different interpretations of what constitutes a delivery. As noted in chapter 2, governments have some discretion in defining when a delivery takes place. If parties have a different view, a number of items may be reported differently, especially if the transfer occurs around the end of one year or the beginning of another.

An example is the report by Germany on the transfer of a conventional submarine to South Korea. This is reported by Germany as an export but not by South Korea as an import. The necessary documentation was signed in 1992—making this a transfer in the eyes of Germany. However, the ship was still undergoing sea trials in the North Sea and the Baltic Sea in early 1993—flying German colours and still in the hands of the shipyard which built it. The ship was not commissioned into the South Korean Navy until January 1993 and presumably will appear in the 1993 South Korean return to the UN but not in that of Germany. In the SIPRI register the Korean approach is taken and delivery of the ship will not be recorded until 1993. These kinds of problem can only be prevented by adopting a standard definition of an arms transfer.

In a surprising category there are records which match but which, strictly speaking, should not match. These matches are created if governments go beyond the UN Register categories in their reports. For example, in its export return Germany reports the delivery of a warship to India in 1992 as does the SIPRI register. This is an equipment type which would meet the UN Register definition if produced in Germany but which is actually produced in India by the Mazagon Dockyard under a German licence.

Class 3: agreement on a deal but not on number of items

The third class includes cases in which the importing government, exporting government and SIPRI all agree that a certain category or type of weapon has been delivered in 1992 but the difference between their records of numbers delivered is greater than 10 per cent.

If shipments or stocks ready for shipment occur around the end of the year, equipment can go 'missing' from the perspective of one or the other register, with the exporter announcing a transfer but the importer not having received it.

Finding definitive sources on the distribution of deliveries over time is one of the greatest problems faced in compiling SIPRI data. Annexe 2 indicates that many delivery figures (those given within brackets) are estimates. Deliveries reported to the UN in 1992 may either be partly or entirely listed as 'on order' in the SIPRI register or be recorded as delivered before 1992. An example of the first case is the export by the USA of 150 M-113 armoured personnel carriers (APCs) to Greece. SIPRI estimated 50 to have been delivered in 1992, with the other deliveries still pending. Greece and the USA both report that all 150 APCs were delivered in 1992. An example of a delivery having been reported too early by SIPRI is the transfer of 36 second-hand A-4 Skyhawk aircraft from the USA to Argentina. The sale of these aircraft at the end of 1992 was widely reported and delivery was included in the SIPRI register in the *SIPRI Yearbook 1993*. However, they do not appear in the Argentinian or US return to the UN Register, and it seems that delivery will actually occur in 1993 (as new sources available in 1993 also report).

Many of these delivery problems will be eliminated once the UN Register has been in operation for three or four years and a time series has been built up. This will also allow the retroactive correction of the SIPRI register.

Class 4: records contained only in the UN Register

These are transfers reported by an importer, an exporter or both, but not by SIPRI. It is here that the UN Register comes into its own and makes a true contribution to greater 'transparency'. There are four convincing explanations for these types of record.

1. The first is that the item is of a type not counted by SIPRI in its classification. These cases occur in the UN Register category of missiles and missile launchers, where unguided rockets with a range of over 25 km are reported. These are not part of the SIPRI data base. For example, Brazil reports 50 328 SS-30 and SS-60 ASTROS rockets as exports to Saudi Arabia. In this case, as with RP/C M-26/28 deliveries from Germany, designations were given, but had this not been the case a comparison between SIPRI and the UN would produce a very distorted picture. The US transfer of 1212 missile and missile launcher category items to Bahrain can safely be counted as mainly the sale of MLRS rockets because Bahrain has no requirement for more than a handful of long-range guided missiles, but it is difficult to interpret the delivery of 1164 missile and missile launcher category items to Turkey. It is unlikely that they are all long-range guided missiles, and a large proportion might also be MLRS rockets, but that assumption cannot be made with complete certainty.

2. A second explanation could be one noted above—SIPRI has erroneously recorded delivery of the items before 1992 or has them still pending delivery for lack of sources indicating delivery in 1992. As shown in annexe 2, this is a common case and the UN Register will lead to the correction of the SIPRI data.

3. The third possibility is that a transfer has not been reported, or has been reported only vaguely, in the sources on which the SIPRI

data base relies. Here the UN Register has shed new light in confirming deals such as the Italian export of 155-mm guns to Nigeria as well as generating some completely new information. The main revelations in the UN Register came in the reporting of land systems, a category recognized by SIPRI as difficult to track: Romania reported artillery and armoured combat vehicle deliveries to Moldova; Bulgaria gave details of a delivery of 210 artillery pieces to Syria; and China reported deliveries of 106 artillery pieces to Iran. In the past, these countries have closely guarded information on their exports; the UN Register provides the first public record of these transfers. However, even France, whose exports are traditionally better covered in the open sources, reported the previously undisclosed delivery of 175 artillery pieces to Saudi Arabia.

4. The fourth explanation is that some countries reported systems that meet the UN Register criteria but which are not for military service. The UK included in its report several transfers with the comment 'Obsolete equipment for museums', confirming that civil servants are not without a sense of humour. SIPRI, while having a sense of humour, nevertheless does not report such transfers.

Class 5: records contained only in the SIPRI register

These are cases where SIPRI reports a transfer, but neither importer nor exporter gives this information in its return to the UN. Deals which refer to weapon types included in the SIPRI definition of major conventional weapons but which clearly fall outside the scope of the seven UN Register categories are of course excluded from this group of cases. However, there are some clear-cut cases in which transfers of items falling within the UN Register categories are recorded in several sources—including official government statements and with photographic evidence of delivery—but are not reported to the UN.

There are five possible explanations for these cases. One could again be the problem of delivery years noted above. A second could be that neither the exporting nor importing country submitted a report to the UN, as in the case of North Korean missiles to Syria, but there are only a few cases for which this explanation may be valid. A third might be that SIPRI is wrong and has reported a transfer that never took place. However, a fourth explanation is more likely. This is con-

nected with the freedom which the reporting countries have to determine whether or not a weapon fits a UN Register category.

Most of these cases involve trainer aircraft or helicopters, and here a
'grey area' is forming as a result of the discretion which governments
have in deciding whether or not certain systems meet the conditions
of the UN Register categories. According to the combat aircraft and
attack helicopter categories, all aircraft or helicopters specially
equipped to deliver ordnance should be reported and only basic train-
ers or non-combatant transport and utility versions excluded.

In 1992 Switzerland delivered PC-9 trainer aircraft to Thailand,
Brazil delivered EMB-312 Tucano trainer aircraft to Colombia, and
Czechoslovakia delivered L-59 jet trainer aircraft to Egypt. None of
these deliveries has been reported to the UN Register either by the
exporter or the importer. In the category attack helicopters, aircraft
configured for anti-submarine warfare (ASW) seem to have been
'forgotten' although they fall within the UN Register definition since
they are capable of carrying weapons and have an integrated target-
acquisition and designation system. The problem here may be that the
term 'attack helicopter' in normal usage describes a heavily armed
helicopter and not those armed only with machine-guns or unguided
rockets nor those fitted with ASW weapons. For example, neither the
USA nor the Philippines reported deliveries of Model-530MG and
500D helicopters in 1992, even though sources are certain that these
occurred and that they were armed versions.

The weapons in this 'grey area' cannot truly be seen as a major
threat to neighbouring countries but certainly can have a high pro-
file—they are an important tool in counter-insurgency operations, as
witnessed in Iraq, Guatemala and Myanmar where Swiss-produced
PC-7s and PC-9s have been used extensively in an armed role.

The fifth explanation is that governments are cheating. However,
there is no indication that this has happened. All the discrepancies
between government export or import returns to the UN Register and
the SIPRI register can be explained logically.

IV. Evaluating the UN Register

Based on the first year of reporting, has the UN Register been a success in terms of new information about the trade in major conventional weapons? Although it was perhaps not a complete success,

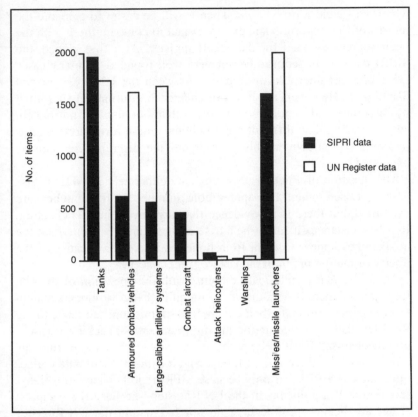

Figure 4.2. Comparison of SIPRI and UN data

Note: Based on exporters' listing and not counting reported systems that do not fit the UN Register or SIPRI definitions.

with 78 countries responding, including all the leading major weapon exporters, the expectations of many were certainly met.

The Register yielded only a few real surprises, but they were significant. The main gain in transparency from the SIPRI point of view was the added information about the scale and timing of transfers whose broad outline was already known from public sources and official confirmation of those transfers, which will also make it easier in the future to make governments accountable for their trade.

In many cases, however, it is too early to judge the importance of many returns to the UN. To do this requires a few years of reporting, which will yield a time series. Then it will be easier to compare the returns of the importers and exporters and to compare these with the open sources as used for the SIPRI register. At a first glance, the SIPRI data might seem to be not very well founded. In many cases there is a considerable discrepancy between the UN Register and SIPRI data. However, as shown in chapter 3, information submitted by importers and exporters more often than not also did not match, again showing how difficult it is to obtain solid information on arms transfers. As shown in this chapter, all the discrepancies can be explained.

The question of whether countries are deliberately providing false data is raised when the appreciable number of mismatches are examined, but there is no evidence that any government is cheating. In a few instances it might be a case of stretching the limits, but the mismatches appear to stem from honest mistakes or because of the liberty of interpretation in the UN Register concept.

There are many technical problems with the operation of the UN Register and there is of course the possibility that governments may in future years co-ordinate their data before submissions are made to the Register, thereby jeopardizing the important cross-checking verification mechanism. Even if the problems are ironed out and governments report honestly, there will still be a role for independent data collections such as SIPRI's, if only because SIPRI reports many arms transfers that will not appear in the UN Register—because the weapons either are licence produced or do not fall within the UN Register weapon categories (see annexe 2 for the SIPRI register for 1992 and the UN Register status for the deal). However, governments will at last have made a commitment to openness and accountability.

5. Conclusions

I. Results of the first year of reporting

The 1991 UN report summarized the purpose of the promotion of transparency in armaments and thus the UN Register of Conventional Arms as 'the building of confidence and security, the reduction of suspicions, mistrust and fear, restraint on a unilateral and multilateral basis, and the timely identification of trends in arms transfers'.[1] The 78 government submissions for 1992 are the first step towards this goal. One year of reporting is, of course, too short a period to draw definitive conclusions on the success or failure of this long-term exercise in transparency. Compared to the wider goals of enhancing peace and stability, increasing openness and confidence, and supporting restraint in arms imports and exports, the first reports are, by definition, only a modest step.

There are two quantitative measures to evaluate the success of the first year of the Register: the extent of participation in the exercise expressed (a) as a proportion of the total number of UN member states and (b) as a proportion of the global arms trade covered. The first aim—to achieve broad participation—has only partially been met with the 78 national returns.

The results regarding the second aim—to achieve reports on most of the global trade in conventional arms—are more positive. All the major exporters except North Korea and South Africa have reported. However, several of the major importers (particularly from the Middle East and Asia) did not participate. The bulk of the entries for 1992 was concentrated among a few suppliers and recipients. A large number of countries had only a few items to report in the UN Register, and many countries reported that they had no data to submit in the seven weapon categories.

Since the UN Register is a new instrument, it is not surprising that it was received with varying degrees of enthusiasm. Initial hesitation or difficulties stemmed from several factors. Although the General Assembly voted in favour of the establishment of the Register by an

---

[1] *Study on Ways and Means of Promoting Transparency in International Transfers of Conventional Arms,* UN General Assembly document A/47/301, 9 Sep. 1991, p. 37.

overwhelming majority, the debate among member states signalled that many governments continue to have reservations against the kind of transparency aimed at by the UN Register. Others maintain their reservations because of the exclusion of certain types of weapon (particularly weapons of mass destruction) or the exclusion of arms procurement through national production. In addition, countries need to change national legislation to be able to comply with the UN Register, since arms transfer data are not allowed to be made public in several countries or because contracts between suppliers and recipients contain confidentiality clauses. Arms transfers are not clearly defined in the UN Register. Governments are also left to decide on an individual basis which systems should be classified in the seven categories. As a result of these uncertainties and national discretion, there were difficulties in interpretation of reporting and non-reporting. Finally, the technical difficulties of keeping records in national export control agencies (in countries where such agencies exist) should not be underestimated. This can also be seen in the cross-checking analysis (see chapter 3).

In addition to the information on arms transfers, background information on military holdings, procurement through national production and legislative procedures has been supplied by nearly half of the countries which reported. These kinds of data are planned to be included in the regular procedure of a standardized form of reporting in 1994, after the first two years of implementation of the UN Register.

While much information on arms transfers was publicly known before reports were filed with the UN—although not always as precisely regarding the number of items or delivery years—additional information was revealed. The UN Register revealed some previously unknown transfers. Thus, the Register has already had an impact on improving the knowledge about arms transfers. In contrast, some information about arms deals that is publicly undisputed does not appear in the UN Register. The UN Register threfore raises many unanswered questions. Although the possibility of governments' intentionally withholding information exists, there is no evidence that this has actually occurred. Furthermore, verification through cross-checking of export and import forms revealed that some data are contradictory. Thus, there is room for improvement in reporting and a need to continue public monitoring of arms transfers. Dealing with these discrepancies and uncertainties is a task both for governments in filing their returns for next year and for the Group of Experts who will review the experience of the Register in 1994.

In its present form the UN Register is not a mechanism for regulating the flow of arms—in contrast to other exercises and national arms export legislation. It is intended to inform and to create transparency, and it will hopefully indirectly contribute to restraining the arms trade, although openness in itself will not curb this trade. Critics of the Register have pointed to these limitations and have made the point that the creation of barriers before arms are traded is more important than obtaining knowledge about what occurred in previous years. History tells us that attempts to control the arms trade seem to falter on the central point that rarely can the participants in the control regime agree *before the fact* that a specific transfer will be destabilizing or exacerbate conflict if it occurs. Individual states make such judgements all the time, so it would be wrong to say that there is no restraint on the arms trade. There is and always has been, but it is primarily unilateral in nature.

The UN Register was designed based on the case of Iraq after the 1991 Persian Gulf War, assuming that if such a register had been in place and Iraq and its suppliers had been reporting, the international community would have responded in some way to deter or dissuade Iraq from either further arms acquisitions or threatening its neighbours. Although a significant amount of knowledge was available to regional states and the major powers regarding the Iraqi weapon inventory, little was done to stop the transfers. On the other hand, the lack of critical details on specific characteristics and capabilities may have created misperceptions and a lack of early warning. In any case, it is well known that the 'never again' conclusions reached about Iraq and its arms buildup were clearly *ex post facto*.

II. Expansion of the UN Register

Expansion of the scope of the Register was envisaged in General Assembly Resolution 46/36 L of 1991, and a number of issues have already been taken up by the Conference on Disarmament (CD) in Geneva and will be on the agenda of a Group of Experts that will make recommendations to the 1994 UN General Assembly. Consensus has to be found on the following issues.

Deepening and widening the Register categories

During the deliberations of the UN Panel of Governmental Technical Experts in 1992, states requested that the definitions of the seven categories of weapons be altered. It was proposed to broaden the existing seven weapon categories, to include more details on transfers—such as weapon models or financial arrangements—and, in addition, an entire range of weapons outside the seven categories of conventional arms—such as cluster bombs, precision-guided munitions, remotely delivered mines, fuel-air explosives, electronic warfare equipment, and so on—have been proposed for registration.[2]

Some of these suggestions are obviously intended to improve transparency (e.g., the disaggregation of missiles and missile launchers or inclusion of weapon types or models); other proposals aim at covering more transfers (e.g., lowering the tonnage of ships) or taking into account new technology developments (e.g., precision-guided munitions). Still other proposals try to capture offensive military capabilities (e.g., aerial refuelling aircraft and airborne electronic warfare equipment).

From the perspective of the overall goals of the UN Register, particularly of improving transparency and avoiding a destabilizing accumulation of arms, all these proposals bear certain merit. It is, however, highly unlikely that all of them will be implemented in the second stage of the UN Register. The present seven categories and their definitions were disputed and the compromise found was certainly not satisfactory to all participants.[3] Similar controversial views can be expected in the second phase.

In a paper presented to the January 1993 Tokyo workshop on the UN Register, the Australian Government listed those types of information at which most defence departments and intelligence agencies would draw the line when it comes to sharing information with other governments or the public.[4] These included intelligence capabilities, contingency plans, weapon characteristics, levels of defence readi-

---

[2] For details, see *Report on the Register of Conventional Arms, Report of the Secretary-General,* UN General Assembly document A/47/342, pp. 16–18, reproduced in annexe 3.

[3] For an evaluation, see Wulf, H., in *SIPRI Yearbook 1993: World Armaments and Disarmament* (Oxford University Press: Oxford, 1993), appendix 10F (see annexe 3 for an excerpt from this appendix).

[4] Presentation of Jill Courtney, Government of Australia, 'Promotion of transparency in arms transfers in the Asia/Pacific region', paper presented at the Tokyo workshop on the UN Register, 26–27 Jan. 1993, unpublished manuscript, p. 1.

ness, military operational deployments, war stocks of sensitive items (e.g., missiles), and detailed characteristics of military bases and sensitive support infrastructure. On the other hand, the paper listed some areas where transparency of data should enhance security: to include general strategic assessments, order of battle, defence budgets and financial planning, military exercises, force structure acquisitions, and major arms transfers. Together, these two lists represent an approximation of what governments can be expected to provide and withhold in the future. They remind us that sovereignty and national security are still the primary concerns of states.

Military holdings and procurement through national production

Inclusion of military holdings and procurement through national production was envisaged in Resolution 46/36 L (1991). This was a compromise, and a condition for initiating the first phase of the UN Register, pressed for by a number of developing countries which rejected a transfer register. It is unlikely that this delicate compromise will be questioned again. What is still an open question, however, is the extent of reporting. Will these items be reported in the same seven weapon categories? A number of governments have given, on a voluntary basis, exactly these data under the heading of 'background information' in the first year of reporting. It seems probable that the transfer and procurement categories of weapons will be synchronized.

Weapons of mass destruction

The Egyptian Government has consistently requested the inclusion of weapons of mass destruction in the UN Register, and Resolution 46/36 L tasks the CD (in para. 13) with addressing 'practical means to increase openness and transparency related to the transfer of high technology with military applications and to weapons of mass destruction . . .'. It is unclear to what extent other governments would accept such a proposal. The nuclear weapon states are likely to reject the inclusion of weapons of mass destruction. Referring to implementation of the 1993 START II Treaty and the 1993 Chemical Weapons Convention (CWC), the Government of Argentina proposed at the CD a separate register to accommodate the concerns of both those countries that wish to see weapons of mass destruction reported and those that want to clearly separate conventional weapons from weapons of mass destruction: '[A] parallel register kept by the United Nations and, like the present register of conventional weapons, supplied with information by interested states, would be a practical instrument for transparency and openness. It would be a kind of logbook which would tell us exactly what stage we have reached and how far we have yet to go'.[5]

High technology with military applications

High technology with military applications has been and is of concern in a number of control regimes. To define for the purpose of the UN Register of Conventional Arms which high technology should be registered, let alone verified, is a major endeavour requiring an efficient reporting system far beyond the present relatively simple task of registration. The concern in the above-mentioned control regimes has been to restrict the flow of relevant technologies. Restriction and control are not the aim of the UN Register; at the best, this will be the outcome of transparency. The *ex post facto* reporting concentrates on transfers, holdings and procurement through national production. If these three areas are covered systematically and over a longer period of time, the registration of high technology with military applications is less relevant. A UN register of transfers, holdings and procurement through national production can function as an early-warning mechanism and will indicate which countries are building up or expanding their military research and development (R&D) and production capacities.

Regionalization of the Register

Recognizing the different security situations in different regions of the world, there is scope for expansion in the direction of regional arrangements which might include different weapon categories, the exchange of other security-relevant data such as military doctrines, military manœuvres, and so on. Initiatives have been launched in Latin America by Argentina and in South-East Asia by Malaysia to

[5] Reprinted in Statements made in the Conference on Disarmament during the first part of its 1993 session on agenda item 8: Transparency in armaments, Conference on Disarmament document CD/TIA/INF.2, 12 May 1993, p. 32.

go beyond the global UN Register and promote regionally oriented transparency and confidence-building forums.

Defining excessive and destabilizing accumulations of weapons

This topic falls clearly within the context of the UN Register. The initiatives to define excessive and destabilizing accumulations of weapons have been futile in the past. The criteria applied, threat perceptions of governments and security situations in the different regions are so vastly different that it is hard to imagine a consensus developing among all the UN member states. Since the UN Register has no monitoring or verification mechanism, it seems practical not to get bogged down in an endless rhetorical tangle. Instead, states are free to take up their concerns in bilateral discussions based on the data which the UN Register provides and not on abstract definitions of 'excessive and destabilizing' arms transfers. Eventually, if such an exchange proves fruitful, discussions could be transformed into formal procedures, for example, along the lines of the General Agreement on Tariffs and Trade (GATT) panels in which governments can request to take up issues of their concern (such as unfair trading practices in the case of GATT).

The expansion of the scope of the Register and thus its future depends on the political will of the UN member states. A number of governments are prepared to make the second stage a bold step. Others are still reluctant. In the words of Ambassador Wagenmakers, 'Some states may view the register, not as a floor or first building block, but as a ceiling—the minimum effort that may make reductions in arms unnecessary. Such risks are real, given the fact that this approach is still in its infant stages'.[6]

---

[6] Wagenmakers , H., 'The UN Register of Conventional Arms: a new instrument for cooperative security', *Arms Control Today*, Apr. 1993, p. 21 (see annexe 3 for an excerpt from this article).

Annexe 1. Returns to the UN Register of Conventional Arms for arms transfers in 1992 compared with SIPRI data

Country	Form	Category[a]	Second country[b]	No. of items	State of origin	SIPRI status[c]	Description/comments[d]
Argentina	Exports	Cbt Acft	Sri Lanka	4	Argentina	Conf.	IA-58 Pucara aircraft/For use as advanced training aircraft by Sri Lankan AF
Austria	Exports	LCA	Thailand	18	..	NR	155mm
Belarus	Exports	Tank	North Korea	19	Russia	NR	870
Belarus	Exports	Tank	Oman	5	Russia	NR	870
Brazil	Exports	M/Ml[e]	Qatar	384	..	NC	SS30, SS60 rockets for ASTROS II
Brazil	Exports	M/Ml[e]	Saudi Arabia	50 328	..	NC	SS30, SS40, SS60 rockets for ASTROS II
Bulgaria	Exports	LCA	Syria	210	..	NR	..
Bulgaria	Exports	Cbt Acft	Russia	3	..	NR	..
Canada	Exports	ACV	Saudi Arabia	262	..	Diff.	Wheeled APC
Canada	Exports	LCA	Italy	2	Italy	NC	OTO Melara 127/54 ship-mounted gun/Originally imported from Italy; returned as partial payment for overhaul of 7 105mm howitzers
China	Exports	Tank	Pakistan	97	..	NV	..
China	Exports	ACV	Sri Lanka	2	..	NR	..
China	Exports	LCA	Bangladesh	42	..	NR	..
China	Exports	LCA	Iran	106	..	NR	..
China	Exports	LCA	Sudan	18	..	NR	..
China	Exports	Ship	Thailand	2	..	Conf.	..
China	Exports	M/Ml	Thailand	24	..	Diff.	..
Czech Republic	Exports	LCA	Zimbabwe	20	..	NR	122mm MRL on wheel chassis Type RM-70
Egypt	Exports	ACV	Algeria	53	..	NR	Wheeled APC with no additional equipment and without armaments

Country		Category	Recipient	Number		Status	Description
Egypt	Exports	LCA	Rwanda	6	:	NR	122mm howitzer
Finland	Exports	ACV	Sweden	2	:	NR	XA-180
France	Exports	ACV	Morocco	14	:	NR	:
France	Exports	ACV	Oman	4	:	NR	:
France	Exports	ACV	Qatar	12	:	NR	:
France	Exports	ACV	UAE	6	:	NR	:
France	Exports	LCA	Saudi Arabia	175	:	NR	:
France	Exports	LCA	Singapore	26	:	Diff.	:
France	Exports	Cbt Acft	Greece	12	:	Conf.	:
France	Exports	Cbt Acft	Venezuela	4	:	Diff.	:
France	Exports	Atk Helo	Chile	1	:	Diff.	:
France	Exports	M/Ml	Brazil	12	:	NR	:
France	Exports	M/Ml	Greece	8	:	NV	:
France	Exports	M/Ml	Saudi Arabia	6	:	NV	:
Germany	Exports	Tank	Belgium	2	:	NR	T-55, T-72
Germany	Exports	Tank	Canada	8	:	NR	T-72
Germany	Exports	Tank	Finland	97	:	Conf.	T-72
Germany	Exports	Tank	Norway	16	:	Diff.	Leo-1
Germany	Exports	Tank	Sweden	6	:	NR	1 Leo-2, 5 T-72
Germany	Exports	Tank	Turkey	11	:	Diff.	Leo-1
Germany	Exports	ACV	Belgium	2	:	NR	BTR-70, BMP-1
Germany	Exports	ACV	Finland	3	:	NR	MT-LB
Germany	Exports	ACV	Greece	3	:	NR	BMP, MT-LB
Germany	Exports	ACV	Sweden	5	:	NR	MT-LB
Germany	Exports	ACV	Turkey	105	:	Conf.	BTR-60
Germany	Exports	ACV	USA	18	:	Conf.	APC Fuchs
Germany	Exports	LCA	Belgium	2	:	NR	Armoured howitzer 122mm
Germany	Exports	LCA	Finland	447	:	Diff.	Armoured howitzer 122mm, 152mm
Germany	Exports	Cbt Acft	Belgium	2	:	NR	MiG-21, MiG-23
Germany	Exports	Cbt Acft	Turkey	11	:	Diff.	Phantom/RF-4E

Country	Form	Category[a]	Second country[b]	No. of items	State of origin	SIPRI status[c]	Description/comments[d]
Germany	Exports	Atk Helo	USA	1	..	NR	Mi-24
Germany	Exports	Ship	Greece	8	..	Conf.	Landing craft
Germany	Exports	Ship	India	1	..	Diff.	Submarine (kit)
Germany	Exports	Ship	South Korea	1	..	Diff.	Submarine
Germany	Exports	M/MI	France	3 852	..	NC	Missiles RP/C M-26
Germany	Exports	M/MI	France	522	..	NC	Missiles RP/C M-28 (test missiles)
Germany	Exports	M/MI	Italy	960	..	NC	Missiles RP/C M-26
Germany	Exports	M/MI	Italy	240	..	NC	Missiles RP/C M-28 (test missiles)
Germany	Exports	M/MI	Sweden	8	..	NC	A/S missiles S-5
Germany	Exports	M/MI	UK	6 888	..	NC	Missiles RP/C M-26
Germany	Exports	M/MI	UK	888	..	NC	Missiles RP/C M-28 (test missiles)
Germany	Exports	M/MI	USA	182	..	Conf.	Guided missiles
Greece	Exports	ACV	Cyprus	49	..	Diff.	Leonidas
India	Exports	ACV	Maldives	2	UK	NR	..
India	Exports	ACV	Maldives	2	USSR	NR	..
Israel	Exports	ACV	Botswana	4	..	NR	..
Israel	Exports	ACV	USA	1	USA	NR	..
Israel	Exports	LCA	USA	1	USA	NR	..
Israel	Exports	M/MI	USA	40	..	Diff.	..
Italy	Exports	LCA	Nigeria	9	..	NR	Self-propelled guns 155mm, 39 calibre
Italy	Exports	Cbt Acft	New Zealand	6	..	Conf.	MB-339C
Italy	Exports	Cbt Acft	UAE	1	..	NR	MB-339C/Replacement
Italy	Exports	Atk Helo	Belgium	10	..	Diff.	A-109 MKII Scout
Italy	Exports	M/MI	USA	2	..	NR	S.S. OTOMAT MKII (improved version)
Italy	Exports	M/MI	Venezuela	6	..	NR	S.S. OTOMAT MKII
Netherlands	Exports	Tank	Greece	100	Germany	Diff.	Leopard 1-V/CFE Treaty cascade
Netherlands	Exports	ACV	Greece	53	USA	NR	M-106
Netherlands	Exports	ACV	Portugal	6	..	Diff.	YP-408 APCCO/NATO Defence Assistance

Exporter		Category	Recipient	No.		Supplier	Status	Comments
Netherlands	Exports	ACV	Portugal	22	..	USA	Diff.	YP-408 ACPI/CFE Treaty cascade/NATO Defence Assistance
Netherlands	Exports	LCA	Greece	171	..	USA	NR	M-30 (4.2" mortar)/CFE Treaty cascade
Poland	Exports	ACV	Latvia	2	..	..	NR	..
Romania	Exports	LCA	Cameroon	12	..	..	NR	130mm gun
Romania	Exports	LCA	Moldova	51	..	..	NR	Amphibious armoured carrier
Romania	Exports	LCA	Moldova	30	..	..	NR	120mm launcher
Romania	Exports	LCA	Moldova	18	..	..	NR	122mm howitzer
Romania	Exports	LCA	Nigeria	5	..	..	NR	122mm/40 MLRS
Romania	Exports	LCA	Nigeria	4	..	..	NR	130mm gun
Russia	Exports	Tank	Oman	6	..	..	NR	..
Russia	Exports	Tank	UK	1	..	..	NR	..
Russia	Exports	ACV	Finland	84	..	..	NR	..
Russia	Exports	ACV	Sierra Leone	4	..	..	NR	..
Russia	Exports	ACV	UAE	80	..	..	Diff.	..
Russia	Exports	ACV	Uzbekistan	30	..	..	NR	..
Russia	Exports	Cbt Acft	China	20	..	..	Diff.	..
Russia	Exports	Cbt Acft	China	6	..	..	Diff.	/Training aircraft
Russia	Exports	Ship	Iran	1	..	..	Conf.	..
Russia	Exports	Ship	Finland	1	..	..	NR	/Leased without arms as a museum piece
Russia	Exports	Ship	Poland	3	..	..	NR	/Payment for warship leased to Poland in 1991
Russia	Exports	M/Ml	China	144	..	..	Diff.	..
Slovakia	Exports	Tank	Syria	81	..	Slovakia	Diff.	Tanks T-72/Contract from 1991
Sweden	Exports	Ship	Australia	:	..	..	Diff.	Submarine sections
Sweden	Exports	M/Ml	Finland	5	..	..	Diff.	RBS-15 system
UK	Exports	Tank	Nigeria	25	..	..	Conf.	..
UK	Exports	Tank	Switzerland	6	..	Czechosl.	NR	/Obsolete equipment for museums
UK	Exports	ACV	Australia	8	..	..	NR	/Obsolete equipment for museums
UK	Exports	ACV	Brunei Darussalam	6	..	Brunei Dar.	NR	/Return of equipment after refurbishment
UK	Exports	ACV	Papua New Guinea	1	..	..	NR	..

Country	Form	Category[a]	Second country[b]	No. of items	State of origin	SIPRI status[c]	Description/comments[d]
UK	Exports	ACV	Saudi Arabia	29	..	Diff.	..
UK	Exports	ACV	Switzerland	1	..	NR	/Obsolete equipment for museums
UK	Exports	ACV	USA	1	USA	NR	/Obsolete equipment for museums
UK	Exports	LCA	Brazil	4	..	Conf.	..
UK	Exports	LCA	Switzerland	1	..	NR	/Obsolete equipment for museums
UK	Exports	Cbt Acft	India	3	..	NR	..
UK	Exports	Cbt Acft	South Korea	10	..	Diff.	..
UK	Exports	Cbt Acft	Saudi Arabia	1	..	NR	..
UK	Exports	Cbt Acft	Zimbabwe	5	..	Diff.	..
UK	Exports	Ship	Chile	1	..	Conf.	..
UK	Exports	M/Ml	Saudi Arabia	48	..	Diff.	..
UK	Exports	M/Ml	UAE	398	..	NR	..
USA	Exports	Tank	Egypt	75	..	Diff.	..
USA	Exports	Tank	Greece	492	..	NR	..
USA	Exports	Tank	Singapore	1	..	Diff.	..
USA	Exports	Tank	Spain	96	..	Diff.	..
USA	Exports	Tank	Turkey	577	..	Diff.	..
USA	Exports	ACV	Bahrain	101	..	NR	..
USA	Exports	ACV	Canada	21	..	NR	..
USA	Exports	ACV	Denmark	2	..	Diff.	..
USA	Exports	ACV	Greece	150	..	NR	..
USA	Exports	ACV	Oman	2	..	Diff.	..
USA	Exports	ACV	Saudi Arabia	192	..	NR	..
USA	Exports	ACV	Thailand	18	..	Diff.	..
USA	Exports	ACV	Turkey	220	..	Diff.	..
USA	Exports	LCA	Bahrain	19	..	Diff.	..
USA	Exports	LCA	Greece	72	..	Conf.	..
USA	Exports	LCA	Turkey	75	..	Diff.	..

USA	Exports	Cbt Acft	Chile	10	..	Conf.
USA	Exports	Cbt Acft	Ecuador	4	..	NR
USA	Exports	Cbt Acft	Egypt	21	..	Diff.
USA	Exports	Cbt Acft	Greece	16	..	NV
USA	Exports	Cbt Acft	Israel	40	..	Diff.
USA	Exports	Cbt Acft	South Korea	1	..	Diff.
USA	Exports	Cbt Acft	Kuwait	23	..	Diff.
USA	Exports	Cbt Acft	Netherlands	2	..	Diff.
USA	Exports	Cbt Acft	Philippines	9	..	Diff.
USA	Exports	Cbt Acft	Saudi Arabia	10	..	Conf.
USA	Exports	Cbt Acft	Turkey	29	..	NR
USA	Exports	Atk Helo	Turkey	6	..	Diff.
USA	Exports	Ship	Greece	1	..	Diff.
USA	Exports	M/MI	Australia	26	..	NV
USA	Exports	M/MI	Bahrain	1 212	..	NV
USA	Exports	M/MI	Canada	88	..	NV
USA	Exports	M/MI	Egypt	3	..	NV
USA	Exports	M/MI	Germany	50	..	NV
USA	Exports	M/MI	Greece	120	..	NV
USA	Exports	M/MI	Italy	8	..	NV
USA	Exports	M/MI	Japan	109	..	NV
USA	Exports	M/MI	Netherlands	80	..	NV
USA	Exports	M/MI	Portugal	19	..	NR
USA	Exports	M/MI	Spain	9	..	NV
USA	Exports	M/MI	Turkey	1 164	..	NV
Australia	Imports	M/MI	USA	29	..	Diff.

/Includes Harpoon, Sparrow and Standard missiles and also 2 MK-13 launchers for fitting to Australian frigates *Melbourne* and *Newcastle*; 2 of the missiles were delivered in a telemetry (training) configuration

Country	Form	Category[a]	Second country[b]	No. of items	State of origin	SIPRI status[c]	Description/comments[d]
Belgium	Imports	Tank	Germany	1	GDR	NR	T-55/Already provided in the global figures contained in the UN Register
Belgium	Imports	Tank	Germany	1	GDR	NR	T-72/Already provided in the global figures contained in the UN Register
Belgium	Imports	ACV	Germany	1	GDR	NR	BMP/Already provided in the global figures contained in the UN Register
Belgium	Imports	ACV	Germany	1	GDR	NR	BTR-70/Already provided in the global figures contained in the UN Register
Belgium	Imports	LCA	Germany	1	GDR	NR	2S1/Already provided in the global figures contained in the UN Register
Belgium	Imports	LCA	Germany	1	GDR	NR	D-30/Already provided in the global figures contained in the UN Register
Belgium	Imports	Cbt Acft	Germany	1	GDR	NR	MiG-21/Already provided in the global figures contained in the UN Register
Belgium	Imports	Cbt Acft	Germany	1	GDR	NR	MiG-23/Already provided in the global figures contained in the UN Register
Belgium	Imports	Atk Helo	Italy	10	..	Diff.	A-109
Bolivia	Imports	LCA	China	36	China	NR	T-54-1/Credit agreement between the governments
Bolivia	Imports	LCA	China	18	China	NR	T-65/Credit agreement between the governments
Brazil	Imports	LCA	UK	4	..	Conf.	105mm light gun
Bulgaria	Imports	Cbt Acft	Russia	5	..	NR	..
Canada	Imports	ACV	USA	22	..	NR	Fully tracked APC
Canada	Imports	M/Ml	USA	5	..	Diff.	Harpoon ship-launched SSMs
Canada	Imports	M/Ml	USA	75	..	Diff.	Sea Sparrow ship-launched SAMs
Chile	Imports	Cbt Acft	USA	10	..	Conf.	Training aircraft designed for counter-insurgency operations/Reported by Chilean AF
Chile	Imports	Ship	UK	1	..	Conf.	Leander Class frigate formerly HMS Ariadne/Reported by Chilean Navy

Country		Category	Source	No.			Description
China	Imports	Cbt Acft	Russia	26	..	Diff.	..
China	Imports	M/MI	Russia	144	..	Diff.	..
Denmark	Imports	ACV	USA	25	..	NR	M-113 A2 MK1 being modified with turret
Denmark	Imports	M/MI	USA	2	..	NV	..
Egypt	Imports	Tanks	USA	26	..	Diff.	/Compartments of battle tanks
Egypt	Imports	Cbt Acft	USA		..	Diff.	..
Finland	Imports	Tank	Germany	97	..	Conf.	T-72 M1
Finland	Imports	ACV	Hungary	1	..	NR	SU-57
Finland	Imports	ACV	Russia	84	..	NR	BMP-2
Finland	Imports	LCA	Germany	447	..	Diff.	..
Finland	Imports	M/MI	Sweden	5	..	Diff.	RBS-15 System
Germany	Imports	M/MI	USA	4	..	NR	Missile launcher
Greece	Imports	Tank	Netherlands	100	..	Diff.	Leo-1V/Imported to replace equal no. of older equipment to be destroyed under CFE Treaty TLE transfer and destruction project
Greece	Imports	Tank	USA	214	..	Diff.	M-60A1
Greece	Imports	Tank	USA	133	..	Diff.	M-60A3
Greece	Imports	ACV	Germany	1	..	NR	BMP-1
Greece	Imports	ACV	Greece	68	..	Diff.	Leonidas/68 ACVs Leonidas procured through national production
Greece	Imports	ACV	USA	150	..	Diff.	M-113
Greece	Imports	LCA	Netherlands	171	..	Diff.	M-30 (4.2")/Imported to replace equal no. of older equipment to be destroyed under CFE Treaty TLE transfer and destruction project
Greece	Imports	LCA	USA	6	..	NR	54 MK-42 (5") gun/Carried by DDG-2 and F-1052 ships (lease)
Greece	Imports	LCA	USA	72	..	Conf.	M-110 A2/Imported to replace equal no. of older equipment to be destroyed under CFE Treaty TLE transfer and destruction project
Greece	Imports	Cbt Acft	France	11	..	Conf.	M-2000

Country	Form	Category[a]	Second country[b]	No. of items	State of origin	SIPRI status[c]	Description/comments[d]
Greece	Imports	Cbt Acft	Germany	5	..	Diff.	RF-4
Greece	Imports	Ship	Germany	4	..	Conf.	Corvettes/Aid
Greece	Imports	Ship	USA	7	..	Diff.	Frigates and DDG/Leasing
Greece	Imports	M/MI	USA	18	..	Diff.	Harpoon missiles/Carried by DDG-2 and F-1052 ships (lease)
Greece	Imports	M/MI	USA	3	..	Conf.	MK-18 launchers
India	Imports	Cbt Acft	UK	3	UK	NR	..
Israel	Imports	Cbt Acft	USA	40	..	Diff.	..
Italy	Imports	LCA	Canada	2	..	NR	Ship-guns OTO 127mm, 54 calibre/Partial repayment for new purchase
Italy	Imports	M/MI	USA	8	..	Diff.	AA type SM-1 - E. R.
Japan	Imports	M/MI	USA	76	..	NV	..
South Korea	Imports	Cbt Acft	UK	10	..	Diff.	Hawk 60/For training purposes only
South Korea	Imports	Cbt Acft	USA	4	..	Conf.	F-16
Lithuania	Imports	ACV	Russia	15	..	NR	Type BTR-60 PA
Lithuania	Imports	Ship	Russia	2	..	Conf.	Light frigate Project-1124
Malta	Imports	Ship	Germany	2	GDR	NC	Bremse patrol boats/Bought for a nominal sum
Malta	Imports	Ship	Germany	2	GDR	NR	Kondor patrol boats/Bought for a nominal sum
Malta	Imports	Ship	Italy	3	..	NC	Ex-Guardia di Finanza patrol boats/Donation
Nepal	Imports	LCA	UK	8	..	NR	105mm field guns
Nepal	Imports	LCA	India	52	..	NR	120mm mortars
Netherlands	Imports	Cbt Acft	USA	2	..	Diff.	F-16 A/C FMS
New Zealand	Imports	Cbt Acft	Italy	6	..	Conf.	Aermacchi MB-339C/New training aircraft but capable of modification
Norway	Imports	Tank	Germany	16	Germany	Diff.	..
Pakistan	Imports	Tank	China	97	..	Diff.	/64 tanks received in 1992, 33 tanks in beginning of 1993
Peru	Imports	Tank	USA	14	..	NR	M-501 light amphibian troop carrier, low mileage/Imported by Peruvian Navy

Country		Category	Supplier	Number		Status	Description
Peru	Imports	ACV	USA	12	..	NR	/Imported by Peruvian AF
Peru	Imports	ACV	South Africa	4	..	NR	Mine-resistant armoured troop carrier, CADOPLA MKIII REPONTEC (personnel carrier for use in jungle areas in anti-terrorist and anti-narcotics traffic operations)/Imported by Peruvian AF
Peru	Imports	Atk Helo	Nicaragua	7	..	NR	Attack helicopter for use in anti-terrorist and anti-narcotics traffic operations/Imported by Peruvian AF
Peru	Imports	Atk Helo	Nicaragua	12	..	NR	/Imported by Peruvian AF
Peru	Imports	Atk Helo	Russia	3	..	Diff.	M5T transport helicopter (helicopter for personnel transport and support for national socio-economic development)/Standard version; imported by Peruvian Navy
Philippines	Imports	Cbt Acft	Russia	19	USA	Diff.	OV-10A
Poland	Imports	Ship	..	3	..	NR	Payment for previously leased warships
Portugal	Imports	ACV	Netherlands	26	..	Diff.	YP-408/Military aid
Portugal	Imports	M/MI	USA	5	..	NR	Harpoon AGM-84-A
Portugal	Imports	M/MI	USA	8	..	NR	Harpoon RGM-84-3
Romania	Imports	Cbt Acft	Moldova	1	..	NR	Fighter MiG-29
Singapore	Imports	ACV	USA	1	..	NR	..
Singapore	Imports	LCA	France	24	..	Diff.	..
Singapore	Imports	M/MI	USA	1	..	NV	Missile
Spain	Imports	Tank	Germany	96	USA	Diff.	M-60/CFE Treaty
Spain	Imports	M/MI	USA	11	..	Diff.	2 MK-13 launchers, 9 Standard Block V missiles/SAM
Sweden	Imports	Tank	Germany	5	..	NR	T-72
Sweden	Imports	ACV	Finland	2	..	NR	XA-180
Sweden	Imports	ACV	Germany	5	..	NR	MT-LB
Turkey	Imports	Tank	Germany	11	..	Diff.	Leopard 1A3/Harmonization
Turkey	Imports	Tank	USA	25	..	Diff.	M-60A1/South Region Aid
Turkey	Imports	Tank	USA	391	..	Diff.	M-60A3/Harmonization
Turkey	Imports	ACV	USA	119	..	Diff.	M-113A2/Harmonization
Turkey	Imports	LCA	USA	69	..	Diff.	M-110 203mm howitzer/Harmonization

Country	Form	Category[a]	Second country[b]	No. of items	State of origin	SIPRI status[c]	Description/comments[d]
Turkey	Imports	Cbt Acft	Germany	11	..	Diff.	RF-4E/Harmonization
Turkey	Imports	Cbt Acft	Netherlands	6	..	NR	NF-5A/Netherlands aid
Turkey	Imports	Cbt Acft	USA	9	..	NR	F-4E/South Region Aid
Turkey	Imports	Atk Helo	USA	6	..	Diff.	AH-1P attack helicopters/South Region Aid
Turkey	Imports	M/MI	USA	24	..	NR	Sea Sparrow guided missiles/FMS
UK	Imports	Tank	Russia	1	..	NR	.. :
UK	Imports	ACV	Brunei Darussalam	2	..	NR	/Equipment imported on a temporary basis for repair and return to country of origin
UK	Imports	ACV	Canada	1	..	NR	.. :
UK	Imports	ACV	Venezuela	7	..	NR	/Equipment imported on a temporary basis for repair and return to country of origin
UK	Imports	LCA	Brazil	2	..	NR	.. :
UK	Imports	LCA	France	14	..	NV	/Obsolete equipment for museums
UK	Imports	LCA	Indonesia	1	..	NR	.. :
UK	Imports	LCA	USA	1	..	NV	/Obsolete equipment for museums
UK	Imports	M/MI	Czechoslovakia	2	..	NV	/Obsolete equipment for museums
UK	Imports	M/MI	Germany	6 888	..	NR	/Obsolete equipment for museums
USA	Imports	Atk Helo	Germany	1	..	NC	.. :
USA	Imports	Ship	Germany	1	..	NR	.. :
USA	Imports	M/MI	Germany	187	..	Conf.	.. :
USA	Imports	M/MI	Israel	40	..	Diff.	.. :
USA	Imports	M/MI	Italy	2	..	NR	.. :

[a] *Abbreviation:*   *UN Register weapon category:*

Tank	I.	Battle tanks
ACV	II.	Armoured combat vehicles
LCA	III.	Large-calibre artillery systems
Cbt Acft	IV.	Combat aircraft
Atk Helo	V.	Attack helicopters
Ship	VI.	Warships
M/Ml	VII.	Missiles and missile launchers

[b] On the exports forms, 'second country' refers to the importer; on the imports forms, it refers to the exporter.

[c] Abbreviations in column for SIPRI status:

Conf.   Confirming the transfer: the entry in the SIPRI register for 1992 is the same or similar to the entry in the UN Register.

Diff.   Different from SIPRI: the transfer is reported in the SIPRI register for 1992 and in the UN Register, but the number of items, the exact designations and/or the delivery years are different, or it is considered as licensed production by SIPRI.

NC   Not counted by SIPRI since it does not fit the SIPRI weapon categories

NR   Not reported in the SIPRI register for 1992 as a delivery or as on order.

NV   Not verifiable because of lack of precise description of equipment in the return to the UN Register.

[d] The wording in the last column is as close as possible to the original text given by governments in their returns to the UN Register.

[e] These were reported to the UN Register as 'large-calibre artillery systems', but for the purpose of this report they are entered as rockets, falling under the UN Register category 'Missiles and missile launchers'.

Annexe 2. The SIPRI register of trade in and licensed production of major conventional weapons, 1992[a]

Importer/ exporter (E) or licenser (L)	No. ordered	Weapon designation	Weapon description	UN category	Year of order/ licence	Year(s) of deliveries	No. delivered/ produced	Of which in 1992	UN Register status[b]
Algeria									
E: China	7	Chui-E Class	Patrol craft	..	1989	1990–92	7	1	Not UN
Angola									
E: Spain	2	C-212-300 Aviocar	Maritime patrol	..	(1990)				..
	4	C-212-300 Aviocar	Maritime patrol	..	1991				..
	(3)	Cormoran Class	Fast attack craft	Ship	1989				..
Switzerland	8	PC-7 Turbo Trainer	Trainer aircraft	Cbt Acft	(1989)	1990	6		..
Argentina									
E: Canada	150	Model 212	Helicopter	..	1990	1992	(4)	(4)	Not UN
USA	36	A-4M Skyhawk-2	Fighter/grd attack	Cbt Acft	1992	1992	36	36	Im/Ex: NR
L: Canada	..	Model-412	Helicopter	..	1991				..
Germany	6	Meko-140 Type	Frigate	Ship	1980	1985–90	4		..
	2	Type TR-1700	Submarine	Ship	1977				..
Italy	..	A-109 Hirundo	Helicopter	..	1988				..
Australia									
E: Canada	97	LAV	APC	ACV	1992	1988–92	(10)	(2)	..
Italy	(10)	HSS-1	Surveillance radar	..	1986				Not UN
Sweden	8	9LV	Fire control radar	..	(1991)				..
	8	Sea Giraffe	Surveillance radar	..	1991				..
UK	(128)	Sea Skua	Anti-ship missile	..	1992				..

	No.	Designation	Description		Year				Comments
USA	4	Boeing-707-320C	Transport aircraft	..	(1990)	1991–92	(4)	(2)	Not UN
	4	CH-47D Chinook	Helicopter	..	1992				..
	18	F-111	Fighter/bomber	..	1992				..
	8	Phalanx	CIWS		1991				
	2	RGM-84A launcher	ShShM launcher	M/MI	1983	1992	1	1	Im: Diff; Ex: NV
	2	RIM-66A launcher	ShAM launcher	M/MI	1985	1992	1	1	Im: Diff; Ex: NV
	8	Sea Sparrow VLS	ShAM launcher	..	(1991)				..
	(128)	NATO Sea Sparrow	ShAM	..	(1991)				..
	(48)	RGM-84A Harpoon	ShShM	M/MI	1987	1992	(24)	(24)	Im: Diff; Ex: NV
	(64)	RIM-67C/SM-2	ShAM	M/MI	(1987)	1992	(32)	(32)	Im: Diff; Ex: NV
L: Germany	10	Meko-200 Type	Frigate	Ship	1989				Not UN; Ex: Conf.
Sweden	6	Type-471	Submarine	Ship	1987				Not UN
UK	129	Hamel 105mm	Towed gun	LCA	(1982)	1987–92	(129)	(16)	Not UN
USA	2	FFG-7 Class	Frigate	Ship	1983	1992	(1)	(1)	Not UN
Austria									
E: Sweden	500	RBS-56 Bill	Anti-tank missile	..	1989	1989–92	(450)	(100)	Not UN
UK	2	BAe-146	Transport aircraft	..	1991				..
USA	24	M-109-A2 155mm	Self-propelled gun	LCA	1988	1989–91	(18)		..
Bahrain									
E: USA	8	AH-64 Apache	Helicopter	Atk Helo	1991				..
	9	MLRS 227mm	MRL	LCA	1990	1992	9	9	Im: NP; Ex: PR—Diff.
	450	AGM-114A Hellfire	Anti-tank missile	..	1990				..
Bangladesh									
E: China	(40)	F-6	Fighter aircraft	Cbt Acft	1992	1992	(40)	(40)	Im: NP; Ex: NR
	(21)	F-7M Airguard	Fighter aircraft	Cbt Acft	1992	1992			..
	2	Hai Ying-2 L	ShShM launcher	M/MI	1988	1989	1		..
	2	Hai Ying-2 L	ShShM launcher	M/MI	1992				..
	(24)	Hai Ying-2	ShShM	M/MI	1988	1989	(12)		..

Importer/ exporter (E) or licenser (L)	No. ordered	Weapon designation	Weapon description	UN category	Year of order/ licence	Year(s) of deliveries	No. delivered/ produced	Of which in 1992	UN Register status[b]
Belgium									
E: France	(8)	Hai Ying-2	ShShM	M/M1	1992				..
	2	Huangfen Class	Fast attack craft	M/M1	1992				..
	2	Jianghu Class	Frigate	M/M1	(1988)	1989	1		..
	714	Mistral	Portable SAM	..	1988	1991–92	(200)	(100)	Not UN
	290	Mistral	Portable SAM	..	1991				..
USA	545	AIM-9M Sidewinder	Air-to-air missile	..	1988				..
	940	AIM-9M Sidewinder	Air-to-air missile	..	1989				..
	(224)	BGM-71A TOW	Anti-tank missile	..	(1989)	1992	(224)	(224)	Not UN
L: Italy	46	A-109A Mk-2	Helicopter	Atk Helo	1988	1992	(30)	(30)	Order incl 28 armed version; Im/Ex: Diff.
Brazil									
E: France	20	AS-550 Fennec	Helicopter	(Atk Helo)	1992	1992	(5)	(5)	Im/Ex: NR; armament uncertain
Italy	..	FILA	Fire control radar	..	(1987)	1989–92	(12)	(3)	Not UN
UK	(7)	Super Lynx	Helicopter	Atk Helo	1991				..
	4	L119 105mm gun	Towed gun	LCA	1991	1992	4	4	Im/Ex: Conf.
L: Austria	..	GHN-45 155mm	Towed gun	LCA	(1985)				..
France	10	AB-565 Panther	Helicopter	Atk Helo	1988	1990–92	10	(3)	Not UN
Germany, FR	..	SNAC-1	Nuclear submarine	Ship	1989				..
	3	Type-209/3	Submarine	Ship	1982				..
Italy	..	MSS-1	Anti-tank missile	..	1986	1988–91	130		..
Singapore	(4)	Grauna Class	Patrol craft	..	1987	1992	2	2	Not UN
UK	..	L119 105mm gun	Towed gun	LCA	1991				..

	No.	Weapon designation	Weapon description		(1970)	1972–92	(1 200)	(30)	Not UN
Brunei Darussalam									
E: Germany	(96)	AIM-9L Sidewinder	Air-to-air missile	..	1989				..
Indonesia	3	CN-235	Maritime patrol	..	1989				..
UK	16	Hawk-100	Jet trainer aircraft	Cbt Acft	1989				..
USA	1	UH-60 Blackhawk	Helicopter	..	(1989)				..
Bulgaria									
L: USSR	..	MT-LB	APC	ACV					Not UN
Canada									
E: Italy	35	EH-101 ASW	Helicopter	Atk Helo	1992				..
Netherlands	4	DA-08	Surveillance radar	..	1986	1991	2		..
	4	LW-08	Surveillance radar	..	1986	1991	2		..
	8	STIR	Fire control radar	..	1986	1991	4		..
	24	STIR	Fire control radar	..	(1985)	1990–92	(6)		Not UN
Sweden	12	Sea Giraffe	Surveillance radar	..	(1985)	1988–92	(3)		Not UN
Switzerland	36	ADATS	SAM system	ACV	1986	1988–92	(21)	(1)	Im: PR—Diff.; Ex: NR
UK	15	EH-101 SAR	Helicopter	..	1992				..
USA	12	AN/SPS-49	Surveillance radar	..	1985	1990–92	(3)	(1)	Not UN
	2	AN/TPS-70	Surveillance radar	..	1990	1992	(1)	(1)	Not UN
	4	Phalanx	CIWS	..	1987	1991–92	(2)	(1)	Not UN
	6	Phalanx	CIWS	..	1986	1988–92	(3)	(1)	Not UN
	6	Phalanx	CIWS	..	1990				..
	12	RGM-84A launcher	ShShM launcher	M/MI	1983	1988–92	(3)	1	Im: NR; Ex: NV
	12	Sea Sparrow VLS	ShAM launcher	..	1983	1988–92	(3)	1	Not UN
	4	Standard VLS	Fire control radar	M/MI	1986	1991–92	2	1	Im: NR; Ex: NV
	3	AGM-84A Harpoon	Anti-ship missile	M/MI	1991	1992	3	3	Im: NR; Ex: NV
	..	RGM-84A Harpoon	ShShM	M/MI	1988	1988–92	(72)	24	Im: Diff.; Ex: NV
	116	RIM-67C/SM-2	ShAM	M(MI	1986	1991–92	(58)	29	Im: NR; Ex: NV
	336	Sea Sparrow	ShAM	..	1984	1988–92	(84)	28	Not UN; Im: Diff.

Importer/ exporter (E) or licenser (L)	No. ordered	Weapon designation	Weapon description	UN category	Year of order/ licence	Year(s) of deliveries	No. delivered/ produced	Of which in 1992	UN Register status[b]
L: France	5 000	Eryx	Anti-tank missile	..	1992				..
UK	40	L-119 105mm	Towed gun	LCA	1990				..
USA	100	Model 412	Helicopter	..	1992				..
Chile									
E: France	4	AS-332 Super Puma	Helicopter	..	1988	1988	2		..
	2	AS-532 Cougar-2	Helicopter	Atk Helo	1992				Ex: PR—Diff.
	12	Mygale	SAM system	..	(1990)	1991–92	(18)	(6)	Not UN
	..	AM-39 Exocet	Anti-ship missile	M/Ml	1992				..
	(1 400)	Mistral	Portable SAM	..	(1990)	1990–92	(600)	(200)	Not UN
Germany	(30)	Bo-105CB	Helicopter	..	1985	1986–92	(18)	(4)	Not UN
Israel	(6)	Barak launcher	ShAM launcher	..	1989				..
	2	Phalcon	AEW&C radar	..	(1989)				..
	(256)	Barak	ShAM	..	1989				..
UK	1	Leander Class	Frigate	Ship	1992	1992	1	1	Im/Ex: Conf.
USA	10	A-37B Dragonfly	Close support ac	Cbt Acft	1992	1992	10	10	Im/Ex: Conf.
	2	Boeing-707	Transport aircraft	..	1991	1992	2	2	Not UN
	2	C-130B Hercules	Transport aircraft	..	1992	1992	(2)	(2)	Not UN
L: South Africa	(400)	G-5 155 mm	Towed gun	LCA	1989	1990	(6)		..
	..	G-6 155mm	Self-propelled gun	LCA	1989	1991	(1)		..
Switzerland	..	Piranha	APC	ACV	1980	1981–92	(249)	(8)	Not UN
UK	..	Rayo	MRL	LCA	1986				..
China									
S: Russia	2	Su-27UB Flanker	Fighter/trainer	Cbt Acft	1992	1992	2	2	Im/Ex: Diff.
USA	6	CH-47D Chinook	Helicopter	..	1989				..

Supplier	No.	Weapon designation	Weapon description		Year(s) of order	Year(s) of deliveries	No. delivered	Comments
USSR	4	AN/TPQ-37	Tracking radar	..	(1987)	1988	2	..
	40	MiG-29 Fulcrum	Fighter aircraft	Cbt Acft	1991			..
	12	Su-24 Fencer	Fighter/bomber	Cbt Acft	(1990)			
	24	Su-27 Flanker	Fighter aircraft	Cbt Acft	1991	1991–92	12	Im/Ex: Diff.
	(144)	AA-10 Alamo	Air-to-air missile	M/MI	1991	1991–92	(72)	Im/Ex: PR
	(96)	AA-8 Aphid	Air-to-air missile	..	1991	1991–92	(48)	Not UN
L: France	(30)	AS-365N Dauphin	Helicopter	..	1992		(552)	..
Israel	..	PL-8H	SAM	..	(1989)	1990–92	(1 385)	Not UN
Colombia								
E: Brazil	2	EMB-110	Transport aircraft	..	1992	1992	2	Not UN
	14	EMB-312 Tucano	Trainer aircraft	Cbt Acft	1992	1992	14	Im/Ex: NR
USA	..	Citation-2	Transport aircraft	..	(1990)	1990	1	..
Cyprus								
E: France	36	AMX-30-B2	Main battle tank	Tank	1989			..
	..	MM-40 CDS	Coast defence sys	M/MI	1989			..
	..	MM-40 Exocet	ShShM	M/MI	1989			..
Greece	75	Steyr-4K 7FA	APC	ACV	(1990)	1990–92	(48)	Im: NP; Ex: Diff.
Czechoslovakia								
L: USSR	..	T-72	Main battle tank	Tank	1978	1981–92	(762)	Not UN
Denmark								
E: France	(9)	TRS-2106 3D	Surveillance radar	..	1991			..
	(9)	TRS-2620	Surveillance radar	..	1991			..
Germany	140	Leopard-1	Main battle tank	Tank	(1991)	1992	(70)	Im/Ex: NR
	6	TRS-3D	Surveillance radar	..	1990	1992	1	Not UN
Sweden	13	9LV	Fire control radar	..	(1988)	1989–92	(7)	Not UN
USA	12	M-110 203mm	Self-propelled gun	LCA	(1991)	1992	(12)	Im/Ex: NR

Importer/ exporter (E) or licenser (L)	No. ordered	Weapon designation	Weapon description	UN category	Year of order/ licence	Year(s) of deliveries	No. delivered/ produced	Of which in 1992	UN Register status[b]
	1	RGM-84A CDS	Coast defence sys	M/MI	1991				..
	162	AGM-65D Maverick	Air-to-surface mis	M/MI	1989				Im: PR—Diff.
	840	FIM-92A Stinger	Portable SAM	..	1991				..
	(24)	RGM-84A Harpoon	ShShM	M/MI	1991				Im: PR—Diff.
Ecuador									
E: UK	3	Jaguar	Fighter/grd attack	Cbt Acft	1991	1992	3	3	Im/Ex: NR
Egypt									
E: Czechoslovakia	48	L-59 Albatross	Jet trainer aircraft	Cbt Acft	1991	1992	(20)	(20)	Im/Ex: NR
USA	24	AH-64 Apache	Helicopter	Atk Helo	1990				..
	2	Commuter-1900	Transport aircraft	..	(1989)	1991–92	2	1	Not UN
	2	E-2C Hawkeye	AEW aircraft	..	1989	1990	1		..
	42	F-16C	Fighter aircraft	Cbt Acft	1987	1991–92	(22)	(12)	Im/Ex: Diff.
	46	F-16C/D	Fighter aircraft	Cbt Acft	1991	1991–92	(40)	(20)	Im/Ex: NR
	40	M-88-A1	ARV	ACV	1990	1991–92			Im/Ex: NR
	492	AGM-114A Hellfire	Anti-tank missile	..	1990		80		..
	144	AGM-65D Maverick	Air-to-surface mis	M/MI	1988	1991			Im/Ex: NR
	40	AGM-65D Maverick	Air-to-surface mis	M/MI	1991	1992	40	40	Im/Ex: NR
	40	AGM-65G Maverick	Anti-ship missile	M/MI	1991	1992	40	40	Im/Ex: NR
	282	AIM-7M Sparrow	Air-to-air missile	M/MI	(1987)	1992	(150)	(150)	Not UN
	695	BGM-71D TOW-2	Anti-tank missile	..	1992	1992	695	695	..
	7 511	BGM-71D TOW-2	Anti-tank missile	M/MI	1988	1989–91	(600)		..
	29	UGM-84A Harpoon	SuShM	M/MI	1990				Not UN
	3	Swiftships MCM	MCM	..	1991				..
L: Germany	..	Fahd	APC	ACV	1978	1988–92	550	(110)	Not UN

Supplier	No. ordered	Weapon designation	Weapon description		Year of order	Year(s) of deliveries	No. delivered		Comments
UK	..	Swingfire	Anti-tank missile	..	1977	1979–92	8 168	(756)	Not UN
USA	(530)	M-1-A1 Abrams	Main battle tank	Tank	1988	1988–92	26	(10)	Im: Diff.; Ex: PR—Diff.
	26	AN/TPS-63	Surveillance radar		1986	1990–92	1 121	(505)	Not UN
	..	AIM-9P Sidewinder	Air-to-air missile	..	(1988)				Not UN
Ethiopia									
E: USSR	1	Natya Class	MCM		(1990)		1		..
	2	Sonya Class	MCM		(1990)		2		..
Fiji									
E: Australia	3	ASI-315	Patrol craft		1992		1		..
France	1	AS-365N Dauphin	Helicopter		1990	1992	1		Not UN
Finland									
E: France	20	Crotale NG	SAM system	..	1990	1992	(10)	(10)	Not UN
	10	TRS-2230/15	Surveillance radar	..	1990				..
	(360)	Mistral	Portable SAM	..	1989	1990–91	(180)		..
	(480)	VT-1	SAM	LCA	1990	1992	(240)	(240)	Not UN
Germany	(290)	D-30 122mm	Towed gun		1992	1992	(290)	(290)	Im/Ex: Diff.
	90	T-72	Main battle tank	Tank	1992	1990–92	4	(90)	Im/Ex: Conf.
Sweden	4	9LV	Fire control radar	..	(1988)	1990–92	4	2	Not UN
	4	Giraffe 100	Surveillance radar		1991		4		..
	4	RBS-15 launcher	ShShM launcher	M/M1	1987	1990–92	(4)	(2)	Im/Ex: PR—Diff.
	64	RBS-15	ShShM	M/M1	(1987)	1990–92	64	32	Im/Ex: PR—Diff.
UK	7	Hawk	Jet trainer aircraft	Cbt Acft	1990				..
	..	Marksman	AAV(G)		1992				..
USA	64	F/A-18 Hornet	Fighter aircraft	Cbt Acft	1992				..
	(128)	AIM-120 AMRAAM	Air-to-air missile	M(M1	1992				..
	(384)	AIM-9M Sidewinder	Air-to-air missile	..	1992				..
France									
E: Brazil	50	EMB-312 Tucano	Trainer aircraft	Cbt Acft	1991				..

Importer/ exporter (E) or licenser (L)	No. ordered	Weapon designation	Weapon description	UN category	Year of order/ licence	Year(s) of deliveries	No. delivered/ produced	Of which in 1992	UN Register status[b]
Germany	(30)	Alpha Jet	Jet trainer aircraft	Cbt Acft	1992				..
Spain	6	CN-235	Transport aircraft	..	1991				..
Switzerland	5	PC-6	Utility aircraft	..	1990	1992	5	5	Not UN
USA	1 000	VT-1	SAM	..	1988	1990–92	(625)	(250)	Not UN
L: USA	55	MLRS 227mm	MRL	LCA	1985	1985–92	(46)	(12)	Not UN
	..	VT-1	SAM	..	1991				..
Gabon									
E: France	(5)	Mygale	SAM system	..	(1990)	1992	(2)	(2)	Not UN
Germany									
E: France	23	TRS-3050	Surveillance radar	..	1987	1987–92	(16)	(3)	Not UN
	200	Apache	Air-to-surface mis	M/M1	1992				..
Netherlands	4	LW-08	Surveillance radar	..	(1989)				..
	5	Smart	Surveillance radar	..	1989				..
	8	STIR	Fire control radar	..	1989				..
USA	10	D-500 Egrett	AEW&C aircraft	..	1992				..
	3	AN/FPS-117	Surveillance radar	..	1988	1991–92	(3)	(2)	Not UN
	5	AN/FPS-117	Surveillance radar	..	1992				..
	4	Sea Sparrow VLS	ShAM launcher	..	1989				Im: PR; Ex: PR
	1 182	AGM-88 Harm	Anti-radar missile	M/M1	1987	1988–92	(900)	(180)	Im: NR; Ex: PR—Diff.
	175	AIM-120 AMRAAM	Air-to-air missile	M/M1	1991				..
	804	MIM-104 Patriot	SAM	..	1984	1989–91	804		..
	(64)	Sea Sparrow	ShAM	..	1989				..
L: USA	150	MLRS 227mm	MRL	LCA	1985	1989–92	120	(35)	Not UN
	..	AIM-120 AMRAAM	Air-to-air missile	M/M1	1989				..

Supplier	No.	Weapon designation	Weapon description	Category	Year of order	Year(s) of deliveries	No.	No.	Comments
	4 500	FIM-92 Stinger	Portable SAM	..	1987	1992	250	250	Not UN
	(1 500)	RIM-116 A RAM	ShAM	..	1985	1989–92	350	(102)	Not UN
Greece									
E: France	40	Mirage-2000	Fighter aircraft	Cbt Acft	1985	1988–92	40	11	Im/Ex: Conf.
	(240)	Magic-2	Air-to-air missile	..	1986	1988–92	(240)	(72)	Not UN
Germany	..	RF-4E Phantom	Recce aircraft	Cbt Acft	(1991)				Im: Diff.; Ex: NR
	150	RM-70 122mm	MRL	LCA	(1991)				..
	75	Leopard-1	Main battle tank	Tank	(1991)	1992	(25)	(25)	Im/Ex: NR
	200	M-113	APC	ACV	(1991)				..
	(64)	NATO Sea Sparrow	ShAM	..	(1988)	1992	(16)	(16)	Not UN
	1	Meko-200 Type	Frigate	Ship	1988	1992	1	1	Im: PR; Ex: NR
	5	Thetis Class	Corvette	..	1989	1991–92	5	3	Not UN; Im: Diff.
	8	Type 520	Landing craft	..	1989	1989–92	(8)	6	Not UN; Ex: Diff.
Netherlands	171	M-30 107mm	Mortar	LCA	(1991)				Im/Ex: Diff.
	170	Leopard-1-A4	Main battle tank	Tank	1991	1992	170	170	Im/Ex: Diff.
	177	M-113	APC	ACV	1991				..
	4	DA-08	Surveillance radar	..	1988	1992	1	1	Not UN
	4	MW-08	Surveillance radar	..	(1989)	1992	1	1	Not UN
	3	RGM-84A launcher	ShShM launcher	M/MI	1992				..
	3	Sea Sparrow launcher	ShAM launcher	..	1992				..
	8	STIR	Fire control radar	..	1989	1992	2	2	Not UN
	3	Kortenaer Class	Frigate	Ship	1992				..
UK	32	F-4 Phantom	Fighter aircraft	Cbt Acft	1992				..
	2	Martello 743-D	Surveillance radar	..	1990	1992	(2)	(2)	Not UN
USA	(36)	A-7E Corsair-2	Fighter/grd attack	Cbt Acft	1991				Ex: PR
	8	AH-64 Apache	Helicopter	Atk Helo	(1991)				..
	5	C-130B Hercules	Transport aircraft	..	(1991)				..
	(40)	F-16C	Fighter aircraft	Cbt Acft	1992				..
	12	P-3A Orion	Maritime patrol	Cbt Acft	1990	1992	12	12	Ex: PR
	5	SH-60B Seahawk	Helicopter	Atk Helo	1991				..

Importer/ exporter (E) or licenser (L)	No. ordered	Weapon designation	Weapon description	UN category	Year of order/ licence	Year(s) of deliveries	No. delivered/ produced	Of which in 1992	UN Register status[b]
	72	M-110 203mm	Self-propelled gun	LCA	(1991)	1992	(72)	(72)	Im/Ex: Conf.
	100	M-30 107mm	Mortar	LCA	1991	1992	(35)	(35)	Not UN
	150	M-113	APC	ACV	(1991)	1992	(50)	(50)	Im/Ex: Diff.
	359	M-60-A1 Patton	Main battle tank	Tank	(1990)	1991–92	(359)	(65)	Im/Ex: Diff.
	312	M-60-A3 Patton	Main battle tank	Tank	(1990)	1990–92	(253)	82	Im/Ex: Diff.
	8	Phalanx	CIWS	..	(1987)	1992	2	2	Not UN
	4	RGM-84A launcher	ShShM launcher	M/MI	1991	1991–92	4	3	Not UN
	4	RGM-84A launcher	ShShM launcher	M/MI	1989	1992	1	1	Im/Ex: NR
	3	RGM-84A launcher	ShShM launcher	M/MI	1992	1992	2	2	Not UN
	4	RIM-67A launcher	ShAM launcher	M/MI	1991	1991–92	4	3	Not UN
	3	Sea Sparrow launcher	ShAM launcher	..	1992	1992	2	2	Not UN
	4	Sea Sparrow VLS	ShAM launcher	..	1988	1992	1	1	Not UN
	446	AGM-114A Hellfire	Anti-tank missile	..	1991				::
	1 500	FIM-92A Stinger	Portable SAM	..	1988	1989–92	(1 000)	(250)	Not UN
	16	RGM-84A Harpoon	ShShM	M/MI	1989	1992	16	16	Im/Ex: NR
	24	RGM-84A Harpoon	ShShM	M/MI	1991	1991–92	(24)	(18)	Im: Diff.; Ex: NR
	(24)	RGM-84A Harpoon	ShShM	M/MI	1992	1992	(16)	(16)	Im: Diff.; Ex: NR
	(64)	RIM-67A/SM-1	ShAM	M/MI	1991	1991–92	(64)	(48)	Im/Ex: NR
	4	Adams Class	Destroyer	Ship	1990	1991–92	4	3	Im: Conf.; Ex: NR
	3	Knox Class	Frigate	Ship	1992	1992	2	2	Im: Diff.; Ex: NR
L: Austria	324	Steyr-4K 7FA	APC	ACV	(1987)	1991–92	120	(60)	Not UN; Im: Diff.
Germany	3	Meko-200 Type	Frigate	Ship	1988				::
India									
E: France	..	PSM-33	Surveillance radar	..	1988	1990–92	(3)	(1)	Not UN
Germany	1	Rajaba Class	Support ship	Ship	1987				::

	No.	Weapon designation	Weapon description	Category	Year of order	Year(s) of deliveries	No. delivered	(No.)	Comments
Russia	20	MiG-29 Fulcrum	Fighter aircraft	Cbt Acft	1992	1992	..		..
	..	2S6	AAV(M)	ACV	1992	1992	..		..
	..	SA-19	SAM	..	1992	1992	..		Not UN
USA	2	AN/TPQ-37	Tracking radar	..	(1990)	1992	(2)	(2)	Not UN
USSR	10	Mi-26 Halo	Helicopter	..	1988	1992	4	1	..
	8	Bass Tilt	Fire control radar	..	1983	1989–91	4		..
	8	SSN-2 Styx L	ShShM launcher	M/MI	1983	1989–91	2		Im/Ex: NR
	6	SSN-2 Styx L	ShShM launcher	M/MI	1987	1991–92			Not UN
	..	AT-4 Spigot	Anti-tank missile	..	1983	1991–92	(600)	1	Not UN
	(400)	SA-16 Gimlet	Portable SAM	..	(1990)	1991–92	(400)	(300)	..
	..	SA-N-5 Grail	ShAM	..	(1983)	1989–91	(160)	(200)	Not UN
	..	SA-N-5 Grail	ShAM	..	1987	1991–92	(80)		..
	(200)	SA-N-5 Grail	ShAM	..	1983	1989–91	(160)	(40)	..
	..	SSN-2 Styx	ShShM	M/MI	1983	1989–91	(48)		..
	..	SSN-2 Styx	ShShM	M/MI	1987	1991–92	(24)	(12)	Im/Ex: NR
	5	Pauk Class	Patrol craft	..	1983	1989–91	4		..

L:	No.	Weapon designation	Weapon description	Category	Year of order	Year(s) of deliveries	No. delivered	(No.)	Comments
France	..	SA-316B Chetak	Helicopter	..	(1962)	1964–92	209	(3)	Not UN
	27 112	Milan	Anti-tank missile	..	1982	1985–92	27 112	2 567	Not UN
	(15 000)	Milan-2	Anti-tank missile	..	1992				Not UN; Ex: Conf.
Germany	103	Do-228	Transport aircraft	(Cbt Acft)	1983	1987–92	46	(10)	Not UN
	2	Type-1500	Submarine	Ship	1981	1992	1	1	Not UN
Korea, South	7	Sukanya Class	Patrol ship	Ship	1987	1990–92	4	1	Not UN
Netherlands	212	Flycatcher	Fire control radar	..	(1987)	1988–92	82	(20)	Not UN
UK	2	Magar Class	Landing ship	Ship	(1979)	1987–92	1	1	Not UN
USSR	(200)	MiG-27 Flogger	Fighter/grd attack	Cbt Acft	1983	1984–92	117	15	Not UN
	..	BMP-2	AIFV	ACV	1983	1987–92	184	(60)	Not UN
	500	T-72	Main battle tank	Tank	(1980)	1987–92	346	(60)	Not UN
	..	AA-8 Aphid	Air-to-air missile	..	(1986)				..
	6	Vibhuti Class	Corvette	Ship	1987	1991–92	2	1	Not UN

Importer/ exporter (E) or licenser (L)	No. ordered	Weapon designation	Weapon description	UN category	Year of order/ licence	Year(s) of deliveries	No. delivered/ produced	Of which in 1992	UN Register status[b]
Indonesia									
E: Germany	(128)	SA-N-5 Grail	ShAM	:	1992				:
	12	Frosch Class	Landing ship	(Ship)	1992				:
	2	Frosch II Class	Support ship	(Ship)	1992				:
	9	Kondor Class	Minesweeper	:	1992				:
	16	Parchim Class	Corvette	Ship	1992				:
Netherlands	:	F-27 Mk-100	Transport aircraft	:	1990				:
UK	(14)	AR-325	Surveillance radar	:	1989	1991–92	(6)	(4)	Not UN
	1	Rover Class	Supply ship	(Ship)	1991	1992	1	1	Not UN
USA	1	B-737 Surveiller	Maritime patrol	:	1991				:
L: France	:	AS-332 Super Puma	Helicopter	:	1983	1985–91	10		:
Germany	(100)	NBo-105	Helicopter	:	1987	1988–92	60	(12)	Not UN
	6	PB-57 Type	Patrol craft	:	1982	1988–92	6	1	Not UN
Spain	(80)	CN-212 Aviocar	Transport aircraft	:	1976	1978–92	40	(4)	Not UN
UK	(14)	Hawk-100	Jet trainer aircraft	Cbt Acft	1992				:
	(10)	Hawk-200	Fighter/grd attack	Cbt Acft	1992				:
USA	:	Model 412	Helicopter	:	1982	1986–91	16		:
Iran									
E: China	(72)	F-7M Airguard	Fighter aircraft	Cbt Acft	(1991)	1992	(18)	(18)	Im: NP; Ex: NR
	(8)	HQ-2B SAMS	SAM system	:	(1989)	1990–92	(6)	(2)	Not UN
	(96)	HQ-2B	SAM	:	1989	1990–92	(72)	(24)	Not UN
	(10)	Hegu Class	Fast attack craft	Ship	(1991)				:
Korea, North	:	Scud-C launcher	Mobile SSM sys	LCA	(1991)	1992	(5)	(5)	Im/Ex: NP
	(170)	Scud-C	SSM	M/MI	(1991)	1992	(100)	(100)	Im/Ex: NP
Russia	2	A-50 Mainstay	AEW&C aircraft	:	1992				:

	No.	Weapon designation	Weapon description		1989/1991	1990–92/1992			Comments
USSR	(500)	T-72	Main battle tank	Tank	1989	1990–92	(200)	(100)	Im: NP; Ex: PR
	2	Kilo Class	Submarine	Ship	1991	1992	1	1	Im: NP; Ex: Conf.
Israel									
E: Germany	1	SA-6 SAMS	SAM system	..	1991				..
	:	SA-6 Gainful	SAM	..	1991				..
	2	Dolphin Class	Submarine	Ship	1991				..
USA	7	AH-64 Apache	Helicopter	Atk Helo	(1992)				..
	(24)	AH-64 Apache	Helicopter	Atk Helo	1992				..
	15	F-15A Eagle	Fighter aircraft	Cbt Acft	1990	1991–92	(15)	9	Im: PR; Ex: NR
	10	F-15A Eagle	Fighter aircraft	Cbt Acft	1991	1992	10	10	Im/Ex: Conf.
	60	F-16C/D	Fighter aircraft	Cbt Acft	1988	1991–92	(30)	(15)	Im/Ex: Diff.
	:	S-65A Stallion	Helicopter	..	(1992)				..
	(10)	UH-60 Blackhawk	Helicopter	..	(1992)				..
	3	RGM-84A launcher	ShShM launcher	M/MI	(1988)				..
	539	AGM-114A Hellfire	Anti-tank missile	..	1990	1990–92	(300)	(100)	Not UN
	300	AIM-9S Sidewinder	Air-to-air missile	..	1990				..
	:	FIM-92A Stinger	Portable SAM	..	1990				..
	(48)	RGM-84A Harpoon	ShShM	M/MI	(1988)				..
	3	Saar-5 Class	Corvette	Ship	1988				..
Ireland									
E: Spain	2	CN-235MPA	Maritime patrol	..	1991	1992	1	1	Not UN
Italy									
E: Germany	8	Do-228-200	Transport aircraft	..	1990	1991	2		..
	:	Kormoran-2	Anti-ship missile	M/MI	(1986)	1990–91	(30)		..
USA	13	AV-8B Harrier 2-Plus	Fighter/grd attack	Cbt Acft	1990	1990			..
	4	AN/FPS-117	Surveillance radar	..	1990				..
	2	RIM-67A launcher	ShAM launcher	M/MI	(1987)	1992	1	1	Im/Ex: NR
	74	AGM-88 Harm	Anti-radar missile	M/MI	1991	1992	(74)	(74)	Not UN
	446	AGM-88 Harm	Anti-radar missile	M/MI	1992				..

Importer/ exporter (E) or licenser (L)	No. ordered	Weapon designation	Weapon description	UN category	Year of order/ licence	Year(s) of deliveries	No. delivered/ produced	Of which in 1992	UN Register status[b]
	(3 900)	BGM-71D TOW-2	Anti-tank missile	..	1987	1990–92	(600)	(240)	..
	(80)	RIM-67C/SM-2	ShAM	M/MI	1987	1992	(40)	(40)	Im: Diff.; Ex: NR
L: France									
USA	..	Aster	SAM	M/MI	1988				..
	..	AB-206B	Helicopter	..	1972	1978–92	(675)	(25)	Not UN
	..	AB-212	Helicopter	..	1970	1971–92	(183)	(3)	Not UN
	..	AB-212ASW	Helicopter	M/MI	1975	1975–91	(105)		..
	..	AB-412 Griffon	Helicopter	..	1980	1982–92	(67)	(3)	Not UN
	50	Model 500E	Helicopter	..	1987	1987–92	(30)	(8)	Not UN
	..	S-61R	Helicopter	..	1990	1991–92	(6)	(4)	Not UN
	22	MLRS 227mm	MRL	LCA	1990	1990–92	(18)	(8)	Not UN
	20	Patriot SAMS	SAM system	..	1985				..
	1 280	MIM-104 Patriot	SAM	..	1988				..
Japan									
E: UK	3	BAe-125-800	Transport aircraft	..	1989	1992	3	3	Not UN
USA	3	BAe-125-800	Transport aircraft	..	1991				..
	3	Beechjet 400T	Transport aircraft	..	1992	1992	3	3	Not UN
	3	E-2C Hawkeye	AEW aircraft	..	1989	1992	3	3	Not UN
	2	E-2C Hawkeye	AEW aircraft	..	1990				..
	2	EP-3C Orion	Elint aircraft	Cbt Acft	1992				..
	36	MLRS 227mm	MRL	LCA	(1991)	1992	9	9	Im/Ex: NR
	1	AN/SPY-1D	Surveillance radar	..	1988	1992	1	1	Not UN
	2	AN/SPY-1D	Surveillance radar	..	1992				..
	6	Phalanx	CIWS	..	1988				..
	3	RGM-84A launcher	ShShM launcher	M/MI	1988				..
	3	Standard VLS	Fire control radar	M/MI	1988				..

75	AGM-84A Harpoon	Anti-ship missile	M/M!	1990	1991–92	(39)	(14)	Im/Ex: NV
32	RGM-84A Harpoon	ShShM	M/MI	1988				..
14	RGM-84A Harpoon	ShShM	M/MI	1992				..
..	RIM-66C/SM-2	ShAM	M/MI	1988	1991	24		Im/Ex: NV
L: France								
..	TB-120mm	Mortar	LCA	1992	1992			..
Italy								
3	Sparviero Class	Fast attack craft	Ship	1990	1990			
UK								
176	FH-70 155mm	Towed gun	LCA	1984	1989–92	125	26	Not UN
USA								
..	CH-47D Chinook	Helicopter	..	(1984)	1986–92	35	3	Not UN
2	EP-3C Orion	Elint aircraft	Cbt Acft	1987	1991–92	2	1	Not UN
55	F-15J Eagle	Fighter aircraft	Cbt Acft	1985	1988–92	48	7	Not UN
(130)	FS-X	Fighter aircraft	Cbt Acft	1988				..
..	Model-205 Kai	Helicopter	..	1991	1992	13	13	Not UN
78	Model 209 AH-1S	Helicopter	Atk Helo	1982	1984–92	65	4	Not UN
135	OH-6D	Helicopter	..	1977	1978–92	144	14	Not UN
70	P-3C Orion	Maritime patrol	Cbt Acft	1985	1987–92	39	1	Not UN
49	SH-60J Seahawk	Helicopter	Atk Helo	1988	1990–92	22	7	Not UN
46	UH-60J Blackhawk	Helicopter	..	1988	1990–92	13	4	Not UN
1 330	AIM-7M Sparrow	Air-to-air missile	M/MI	1990	1990–92	475	170	Not UN
..	BGM-71C I-TOW	Anti-tank missile	..	(1983)	1985–92	4 974	900	Not UN
980	MIM-104 Patriot	SAM	..	1984	1989–92	644	192	Not UN
..	MIM-23B Hawk	SAM	..	1978	1978–92	3 104	(100)	Not UN
Kenya								
E: France								
100	Mistral	Portable SAM	..	1990	1990–92	(60)	(20)	Not UN
Kiribati								
E: Australia								
1	ASI-315	Patrol craft	..	1992				..
Korea, North								
L: China								
..	Romeo Class	Submarine	Ship	1973	1975–92	14	(1)	Not UN

Importer/ exporter (E) or licenser (L)	No. ordered	Weapon designation	Weapon description	UN category	Year of order/ licence	Year(s) of deliveries	No. delivered/ produced	Of which in 1992	UN Register status[b]
Korea, South									
E: France	1 000	Mistral	Portable SAM	..	1992				
Germany	1	Type-209/3	Submarine	Ship	1987				Im: NR; Ex: Diff.
Netherlands	..	Goalkeeper	CIWS	..	1991				..
	1	STIR	Fire control radar	..	(1992)				..
Spain	12	CN-235	Transport aircraft	..	1992				..
UK	20	Hawk	Jet trainer aircraft	Cbt Acft	1990				Im/Ex: Conf.
USA	37	AH-64 Apache	Helicopter	Atk Helo	1992				..
	30	F-16C/D	Fighter aircraft	Cbt Acft	1981	1987–92	(30)	(5)	Im/Ex: Diff.
	48	F-16C/D	Fighter aircraft	Cbt Acft	1991				..
	8	P-3C Update-3 Orion	Maritime patrol	Cbt Acft	1990				..
	90	UH-60 Blackhawk	Helicopter	..	1990	1991–92	(7)	(5)	Not UN
	3	AN/FPS-117	Surveillance radar	..	1990	1992	(1)	(1)	Not UN
	1	RGM-84A launcher	ShShM launcher	M/MI	(1992)				..
	4	Sea Sparrow VLS	ShAM launcher	..	1990				..
	775	AGM-114A Hellfire	Anti-tank missile	..	1992				..
	28	AGM-84A Harpoon	Anti-ship missile	M/MI	1992				..
	40	AGM-88 Harm	Anti-radar missile	M/MI	1992				..
	179	AIM-7M Sparrow	Air-to-air missile	M/MI	1991	1992	(90)	(90)	Im/Ex: NR
	704	BGM-71D TOW-2	Anti-tank missile	M/MI	1987	1990–92	(704)	(204)	Not UN
	(24)	RGM-84A Harpoon	ShShM	..	(1992)				..
	21	Sea Sparrow	ShAM	M/MI	1990				..
L: Germany	2	Type-209/3	Submarine	Ship	1987	1992	1	1	Not UN
	3	Type-209/3	Submarine	Ship	1989				..
	3	Type-209/3	Submarine	Ship	1992				..
Italy	6	Lerici Class	MCM	..	(1986)	1986	1		..

Supplier	No.	Weapon designation	Weapon description	Category	Year of order	Year(s) of deliveries	No. delivered	( )	Comments
Japan	30	BK-117	Helicopter	..	1990		20	(10)	Not UN
USA	72	F-16C/D	Fighter aircraft	Cbt Acft	1991	1991–92	12		..
	(150)	H-76 Eagle	Helicopter	..	1986	1991	100	(50)	Not UN
	250	M-109-A2 155mm	Self-propelled gun	LCA	1990	1991–92	100	(70)	Not UN
	(620)	K-1	Main battle tank	Tank	1980	1985–92	560		Not UN
	..	M-167 Vulcan	CIWS	..	(1986)	1986–91	66		..

Kuwait

E: Australia

Supplier	No.	Weapon designation	Weapon description	Category	Year of order	Year(s) of deliveries	No. delivered	( )	Comments
Australia	2	ASI-315	Patrol craft	..	1992				..
	2	ASI-315	Patrol craft	..	1992				..
Egypt	10	Skyguard SAMS	SAM system	..	1988	1990–92	10	(3)	Not UN
	(320)	Aspide	SAM	..	1988	1990–92	(320)	(96)	Not UN
France	4	MM-40 launcher	ShShM launcher	M/MI	1992				
	..	Mistral	Portable SAM	..	1992				
	(96)	MM-40 Exocet	ShShM	M/MI	1992				
	4	Combattante-4	Fast attack craft	Ship	1992				
Netherlands	4	Goalkeeper	CIWS	..	1992				
USA	40	F/A-18C/D Hornet	Fighter aircraft	Cbt Acft	1988	1991–92	6	5	Im: NP; Ex: Diff.
	256	M-1-A2 Abrams	Main battle tank	Tank	1992				
	125	M-113-A2	APC	ACV	1992				
	52	M-577-A2	APC command post	ACV	1992				
	46	M-88-A1	ARV	ACV	1992				
	1	AN/FPS-117	Surveillance radar	..	1992				
	6	I-Hawk SAMS	SAM system	..	1992				
	1	Patriot SAMS	SAM system	..	1992				
	300	AGM-65G Maverick	Anti-ship missile	M/MI	1988				
	40	AGM-84A Harpoon	Anti-ship missile	M/MI	1988				
	200	AIM-7F Sparrow	Air-to-air missile	M/MI	1988	1992	(50)	(50)	Im: NP; Ex: NR
	120	AIM-9L Sidewinder	Air-to-air missile	..	1988	1992	(30)	(30)	Not UN
	450	MIM-104 Patriot	SAM	..	1992				..

Importer/ exporter (E) or licenser (L)	No. ordered	Weapon designation	Weapon description	UN category	Year of order/ licence	Year(s) of deliveries	No. delivered/ produced	Of which in 1992	UN Register status[b]
	342	MIM-23B Hawk	SAM	..	1992				..
Lithuania									
E: Russia	2	Grisha-3 Class	Frigate	Ship	1992	1992	2	2	Im: Conf.; Ex: NR
	2	Stenka Class	Fast attack craft	..	1992	1992	2	2	Not UN
	2	Turya Class	Fast attack craft	..	1992	1992	2	2	Not UN
Malaysia									
E: France	2	MM-40 launcher	ShShM launcher	M/Ml	1992				..
	..	Mistral	Portable SAM	..	(1991)				..
	(48)	MM-40 Exocet	ShShM	M/Ml	1992				..
Italy	4	Skyguard	Fire control radar	..	1988	1989–92	(4)	(1)	Not UN
Netherlands	2	DA-08	Surveillance radar	..	1992				..
Sweden	2	Sea Giraffe	Surveillance radar	..	1992				..
UK	10	Hawk-100	Jet trainer aircraft	Cbt Acft	1990				..
	18	Hawk-200	Fighter/grd attack	Cbt Acft	1990				..
	2	Martello 743-D	Surveillance radar	..	1990	1992	(2)	(2)	Not UN
	12	DN-181 Rapier	SAM system	..	1988				..
	2	Seawolf VLS	ShAM launcher	..	1992				..
	576	Improved Rapier	SAM	..	1988				..
	(96)	Seawolf-2	ShAM	..	1992				..
	2	Yarrow Type	Frigate	Ship	1992				..
USA	4	B-200T Maritime	Maritime patrol	..	1990				..
Mexico									
E: USA	10	Model 530MG	Helicopter	(Atk Helo)	1992				..

Recipient / Supplier	No.	Weapon designation	Weapon description	Category	Year of order	Year(s) of deliveries	No.	No.	Comments
Morocco									
E: Spain	2	F-30 Class	Frigate	Ship	1991				..
Myanmar									
E: China	12	F-7M Airguard	Fighter aircraft	Cbt Acft	1990	1990–92	(12)	(6)	Im: NP; Ex: NR
	(2)	Y-8	Transport aircraft	..	(1991)				Not UN
	..	PL-2A	Air-to-air missile	..	1990	1990–92	(48)	(24)	Im: NP; Ex: NR
Poland	10	Mi-2 Hoplite	Helicopter	(Atk Helo)	(1992)	1992	10	10	Not UN
	12	W-3 Sokol	Helicopter	..	1990	1991–92	12	(6)	Not UN
Namibia									
E: France	1	Falcon-900	Transport aircraft	..	(1991)	1992	1	1	Not UN
Netherlands									
E: Germany	25	Buffel	ARV	..	1990	1992	(6)	(6)	Not UN
Italy	3	AB-412 Griffon	Helicopter	..	1992				..
USA	4	Patriot SAMS	SAM system	..	1985				..
	8	RGM-84A launcher	ShShM launcher	M/MI	1988	1991–92	3	(1)	Im: NR; Ex: NV
	8	Sea Sparrow VLS	ShAM launcher	..	1985	1991–92	3	(1)	Not UN
	(40)	AGM-84A Harpoon	Anti-ship missile	M/MI	1988				..
	290	AIM-9M Sidewinder	Air-to-air missile	..	1988				..
	256	MIM-104 Patriot	SAM	..	1985				..
	(192)	RGM-84A Harpoon	ShShM	M/MI	1988	1991–92	(72)	(24)	Im: NR; Ex: NV
	(128)	Sea Sparrow	ShAM	..	1985	1991–92	(48)	(16)	Not UN
L: USA	57	F-16A	Fighter aircraft	Cbt Acft	1983	1987–92	(57)	(7)	Im/Ex: Diff.
New Zealand									
E: Australia	2	Meko-200 Type	Frigate	Ship	1989				..
Italy	18	MB-339C	Jet trainer aircraft	Cbt Acft	1990	1991–92	12	6	Im/Ex: Conf.
Netherlands	2	LW-08	Surveillance radar	..	(1991)	1991–92	(2)	(1)	Not UN
Sweden	2	9LV	Fire control radar	..	1991				..

Importer/ exporter (E) or licenser (L)	No. ordered	Weapon designation	Weapon description	UN category	Year of order/ licence	Year(s) of deliveries	No. delivered/ produced	Of which in 1992	UN Register status[b]
USA	2	Sea Giraffe	Surveillance radar	..	1991				..
	2	Phalanx	CIWS	..	1991				..
	2	Sea Sparrow VLS	ShAM launcher	..	1992				..
	..	NATO Sea Sparrow	ShAM	..	(1991)				
Nigeria									
E: Czechoslovakia	27	L-39Z Albatross	Jet trainer aircraft	Cbt Acft	1991	1991–92	(27)	12	Im: NP/Ex: NR
France	12	AS-332 Super Puma	Helicopter	..	1985	1989–90	6	6	
UK	80	MBT Mk-3	Main battle tank	Tank	1990	1991–92	50	(25)	Im: NP; Ex: Conf.
L: USA	..	Air Beetle	Trainer aircraft	..	1988	1988–92	3	2	..
Norway									
E: France	400	Mistral	Portable SAM	..	1990				..
Germany	92	Leopard-1	Main battle tank	Tank	1991	1992	(46)	(46)	Im/Ex: Diff.
	6	Type-210	Submarine	Ship	1982	1989–92	6	1	Im/Ex: NR
Sweden	(9)	Giraffe	Surveillance radar	..	1989	1992	(3)	(3)	Not UN
	(360)	RBS-70	Portable SAM	..	1989	1991–92	(180)	(90)	Not UN
UK	1	SH-3D Sea King	Helicopter	Atk Helo	1989	1992	1	1	Im/Ex: NR
USA	136	M-113	APC	ACV	1991				..
	100	AIM-120 AMRAAM	Air-to-air missile	M/Ml	1989				..
	7 612	BGM-71D TOW-2	Anti-tank missile	..	1985	1987–92	(5 000)	(1 000)	Not UN
Oman									
E: France	2	Crotale NG Navale	ShAM system	..	1992				..
	2	MM-40 launcher	ShShM launcher	M/Ml	1992				..
	(48)	MM-40 Exocet	ShShM	M/Ml	1992				..
	(48)	VT-1	SAM	..	1992				..

Supplier	No.	Weapon designation	Weapon description		Year of order	Year(s) of deliveries	No. delivered		Comments
Netherlands	2	MW-08	Surveillance radar	..	1992				..
UK	4	Hawk-100	Jet trainer aircraft	Cbt Acft	1989				..
	12	Hawk-200	Fighter/grd attack	Cbt Acft	1990				..
	..	Improved Rapier	SAM	..	1992				..
	2	Muheet Class	Corvette	Ship	1992				..
USA	(96)	AIM-9L Sidewinder	Air-to-air missile	..	1990				..
Pakistan									
E: China	98	A-5 Fantan-A	Fighter/grd attack	Cbt Acft	1984				..
	40	F-7M Airguard	Fighter aircraft	Cbt Acft	1988	1992	(20)	(20)	Im/Ex: NR
	40	F-7P Skybolt	Fighter aircraft	Cbt Acft	1992				..
	25	K-8 Karakorum 8	Jet trainer aircraft	Cbt Acft	1987				..
France	12	SA-315B Lama	Helicopter	..	1992		(20)		..
	1	Eridan Class	MCM	..	1992	1992	1		Not UN
	1	Eridan Class	MCM	..	1992	1992	1		..
USA	6	SH-2F/G Seasprite	Helicopter	Atk Helo	1989	1989	3		..
	(20)	M-109-A2 155mm	Self-propelled gun	LCA	1988				..
	..	AN/TPQ-36	Tracking radar	..	(1990)				..
	4	AN/TPQ-37	Tracking radar	..	(1985)	1987–89	(3)		..
	2 386	BGM-71D TOW-2	Anti-tank missile	..	1987				..
L: China	..	T-69II	Main battle tank	Tank	(1989)	1991–92	160	(150)	Not UN; Im/ Ex: PR—Diff.
	..	Anza	Portable SAM	..	(1988)	1989–92	350	(100)	Not UN
	..	Red Arrow-8	Anti-tank missile	..	1989	1990–92	150	(50)	Not UN
France	1	Eridan Class	MCM	..	1992				..
Sweden	..	Supporter	Trainer aircraft	..	1974	1975–92	212	(12)	Not UN
USA	..	LAADS	Surveillance radar	..	(1989)				..
Panama									
E: USA	4	Cape Class	Patrol craft	..	1991	1991	1		..

Importer/ exporter (E) or licenser (L)	No. ordered	Weapon designation	Weapon description	UN category	Year of order/ licence	Year(s) of deliveries	No. delivered/ produced	Of which in 1992	UN Register status[b]
Papua New Guinea									
E: Spain	4	CN-235	Transport aircraft	..	1991	1992	2	2	Not UN
Peru									
E: Czechoslovakia	100	T-55	Main battle tank	Tank	1992	1992	(100)	(100)	Im/Ex: NR
USA	6	B-200T Maritime	Maritime patrol	..	(1990)	1991–92	(2)	(1)	Not UN
USSR	18	Mi-17 Hip-H	Helicopter	(Atk Helo)	1989	1990	14		Im/Ex: NR
Philippines									
E: Australia	3	PC-57M	Patrol craft	..	1990				..
France	3	MM-40 launcher	ShShM launcher	M/Ml	1991				..
	..	MM-40 Exocet	ShShM	M/Ml	1991				..
Italy	36	S-211	Jet trainer aircraft	Cbt Acft	1988	1989–92	(24)	(6)	Local assembly; Im/Ex: NR
Spain	16	SF-260TP	Trainer aircraft	Cbt Acft	1992				..
	3	Cormoran Class	Fast attack craft	Ship	1991				..
USA	22	Model 500D	Helicopter	(Atk Helo)	1988	1990–92	22	8	Im/Ex: NR
	8	Model 530MG	Helicopter	Atk Helo	1992	1992	6	6	Im/Ex: NR
	24	OV-10F Bronco	Close support ac	Cbt Acft	1991	1991	5		Im/Ex: Diff.
	2	Besson Class	Landing ship	(Ship)	1992				..
L: UK	150	FS-100 Simba	APC	ACV	1992				..
Poland									
E: USA	..	PA-34-200T	Transport aircraft	..	1977				..
L: USSR	..	2S1 122mm	Self-propelled gun	LCA	(1980)	1982–91	490		..

Supplier	No. ordered	Weapon designation	Weapon description	Category	Year of order	Year(s) of deliveries	No. delivered	No. produced	Comments
Portugal									
E: Germany	..	LARS 110mm	MRL	LCA	(1991)				..
Netherlands	104	M-113	APC	ACV	1991				..
Netherlands	24	YP-408	APC	ACV	1991				Im/Ex: Diff.
UK	5	Super Lynx	Helicopter	Atk Helo	1990				..
USA	20	F-16A/B	Fighter aircraft	Cot Acft	1990				..
USA	..	Model 205 UH-1H	Helicopter	..	1989				..
USA	..	Model 209 AH-1G	Helicopter	Atk Helo	1989				..
Qatar									
E: France	4	Crotale NG Navale	ShAM system	..	1992				..
France	4	MM-40 launcher	ShShM launcher	M/Ml	1992				..
France	500	Mistral	Portable SAM	..	1990				..
France	(24)	Mistral	Portable SAM	..	1992				..
France	(96)	MM-40 Exocet	ShShM	M/Ml	1992				..
France	..	VT-1	SAM	..	1992				..
Netherlands	4	Goalkeeper	CIWS	..	1992				..
UK	4	Vita Class	Fast attack craft	Ship	1992				..
Romania									
E: Bulgaria	(42)	2S1-122mm	Turret	..	1988	1989–92	(42)	(40)	Not UN
USSR	..	SA-7 Grail	Portable SAM	..	(1978)	1978–92	(375)	(25)	Not UN
L: UK	..	BN-2A Islander	Transport aircraft	..	1968	1969–92	(450)	(10)	Not UN
USSR	..	Yak-52	Trainer aircraft	..	1976	1979–92	(1 620)	(5)	Not UN
Saudi Arabia									
E: Canada	1 117	LAV	APC	ACV	1990				Ex: Diff.
France	3	MM-40 launcher	ShShM launcher	M/ML	1990				..
France	1 200	Mistral	Portable SAM	..	1989	1991–92	(800)	(400)	Not UN
France	(72)	MM-40 Exocet	ShShM	M/Ml	1990				..
France	3	La Fayette Class	Frigate	Ship	1992				..

Importer/exporter (E) or licenser (L)	No. ordered	Weapon designation	Weapon description	UN category	Year of order/licence	Year(s) of deliveries	No. delivered/produced	Of which in 1992	UN Register status[b]
UK	12	BAe-125-800	Transport aircraft	..	1988	1988–92	(12)	(3)	Not UN
	20	Hawk-100	Jet trainer aircraft	Cbt Acft	1988				..
	40	Hawk-200	Fighter/grd attack	Cbt Acft	1988				..
	48	Tornado IDS	Fighter/grd attack	Cbt Acft	1988				..
	(50)	WS-70	Helicopter	..	1988				..
	461	Piranha	APC	ACV	1990	1992	(50)	(50)	Im: NP; Ex: Diff.
	200	ALARM	Anti-radar missile	M/Ml	1986	1991–92	(120)	(60)	Im: NP; Ex: NV
	(480)	Sea Eagle	Anti-ship missile	M/Ml	1985				..
	3	Sandown Class	MCM	..	1988	1991–92	2	1	Not UN
USA	12	AH-64 Apache	Helicopter	Atk Helo	1990	1992	(12)	(12)	Im: NP; Ex: NR
	24	F-15C Eagle	Fighter aircraft	Cbt Acft	1990	1991–92	22	12	Im: NP; Ex: Diff.
	72	F-15XP Eagle	Fighter/grd attack	Cbt Acft	1992				..
	7	KC-130H Hercules	Tanker/transport	..	1990				..
	8	UH-60 Blackhawk	Helicopter	..	1990	1991–92	8	4	..
	8	UH-60 Blackhawk	Helicopter	..	1992				..
	27	M-198 155mm	Towed gun	LCA	1990	1991–92	(27)	(14)	Im: NP; Ex: NR
	150	M-1-A1 Abrams	Main battle tank	Tank	1990				..
	315	M-1-A2 Abrams	Main battle tank	Tank	1990				..
	207	M-113-A2	APC	ACV	1990	1991–92	(207)	(100)	Im: NP; Ex: Diff.
	400	M-2 Bradley	AIFV	ACV	1990	1992	(140)	(140)	Im: NP; Ex: Diff.
	50	M-548	APC	ACV	1991				..
	9	M-577-A2	APC command post	ACV	1990				..
	43	M-578	ARV	ACV	1991				..
	12	M-88-A1	ARV	(ACV)	1990	1992	(12)	(12)	Im: NP; Ex: NR
	(6)	AN/TPS-43	Surveillance radar	..	1985	1987–92	(6)	(1)	Not UN
	8	Patriot SAMS	SAM system	..	1990				..
	14	Patriot SAMS	SAM system	..	1991				..

362	AGM-114A Hellfire	Anti-tank missile	..	1992				..
900	AGM-65D Maverick	Air-to-surface mis	M/ML	1992				..
770	AIM-7M Sparrow	Air-to-air missile	M/MI	1991				..
300	AIM-7M Sparrow	Air-to-air missile	M/MI	1992				..
300	AIM-9S Sidewinder	Air-to-air missile	..	1992				..
4 460	BGM-71D TOW-2	Anti-tank missile	..	1988	1989–92	(2 000)	(500)	Not UN
1 750	BGM-71D TOW-2	Anti-tank missile	..	1990				..
384	MIM-104 Patriot	SAM	..	1990				..
758	MIM-104 Patriot	SAM	..	1991				..
Singapore								
E: France								
20	AS-550 Fennec	Helicopter	Atk Helo	1989	1991–92	(20)	(10)	Im/Ex: NR
36	LG-1 105mm	Towed gun	LCA	1990	1991–92	(24)	(12)	Im/Ex: Diff.
22	AMX-10 PAC-90	AIFV	ACV	1990	1992	(22)	(22)	Im/Ex: NR
22	AMX-10P	AIFV	ACV	(1990)	1991–92	(22)	(17)	Im/Ex: NR
(200)	Milan-2	Anti-tank missile	..	1989	1990–92	(200)	(60)	Not UN
150	Mistral	Portable SAM	..	1992				..
Netherlands								
4	F-50 Enforcer	Maritime patrol	Cbt Acft	1991				..
Sweden								
4	Landsort Class	MCM	..	1991				..
USA								
11	F-16A	Fighter aircraft	Cbt Acft	1992				Im: PR—NV
20	AGM-84A Harpoon	Anti-ship missile	M/MI	1991	1991–92	(240)	(120)	Not UN
(240)	BGM-71C I-TOW	Anti-tank missile	..	1989				..
Spain								
E: France								
840	Mistral	Portable SAM	..	1991	1992	(150)	(150)	Not UN
USA								
8	AV-8B Harrier 2-Plus	Fighter/grd attack	Cbt Acft	1992				..
1	F/A-18 Hornet	Fighter aircraft	Cbt Acft	1990				..
8	S-76C	Helicopter	..	1991	1991–92	6	4	Not UN
6	SH-60B Seahawk	Helicopter	Atk Helo	1991	1992	2	2	Im/Ex: NR
1	TAV-8B Harrier	Fighter/grd attack	Cbt Acft	1992				..
83	M-110-A2 203mm	Self-propelled gun	LCA	1991	1992	(28)	(28)	Im/Ex: NR

Importer/ exporter (E) or licenser (L)	No. ordered	Weapon designation	Weapon description	UN category	Year of order/ licence	Year(s) of deliveries	No. delivered/ produced	Of which in 1992	UN Register status[b]
	100	M-113	APC	ACV	1991				..
	160	M-60-A1 Patton	Main battle tank	Tank	1991	1992	(133)	(133)	Im: Diff. (reported from Germany); Ex: Diff.
	260	M-60-A3 Patton	Main battle tank	Tank	1991	1992	(166)	(166)	Im: Diff. (reported from Germany); Ex: Diff.
	4	RGM-84A launcher	ShShM launcher	M/MI	1988				..
	2	RGM-84A launcher	ShShM launcher	M/MI	1989				..
	2	RIM-67A launcher	ShAM launcher	M/MI	1989				Im: Conf.
	250	AGM-65F Maverick	Air-to-surface mis	M/MI	1989	1990–92	(250)	(50)	Im: NR; Ex: NV
	200	AIM-120 AMRAAM	Air-to-air missile	M/MI	1990				..
	16	RGM-84A Harpoon	ShShM	M/MI	1989				..
	(16)	RGM-84A Harpoon	ShShM	M/MI	1989				..
	150	RIM-67A/SM-1	ShAM	M/MI	(1989)				Im: Diff.
L: UK	4	Sandown Class	MCM	..	(1988)				..
USA	2	FFG-7 Class	Frigate	Ship	1990				..
Sri Lanka									
E: Argentina	4	IA-58A Pucara	Close support ac	Cbt Acft	1992	1992	4	4	Im: NP; Ex: Conf.
Czechoslovakia	(25)	T-55	Main battle tank	Tank	1991	1992	(25)	(25)	Im: NP; Ex: NR
UK	2	HS-748-2	Transport aircraft	..	(1991)	1992	2	2	Not UN
Sweden									
E: France	..	TRS-2620	Surveillance radar	..	1990	1991	(1)		..
USA	1	Gulfstream-4	Transport aircraft	..	1992				..
	2	Gulfstream-4	Transport aircraft	..	1992				..
	700	AGM-114A Hellfire	Anti-tank missile	..	1987	1990–92	(450)	(150)	Not UN

Switzerland

	No.	Weapon designation	Weapon description		Year of order	Year(s) of deliveries	No. delivered	(No. produced)	Comments
E: France	12	AS-332 Super Puma	Helicopter	..	1989	1991–92	(12)	(11)	Not UN
UK	3	Watchman	Surveillance radar	..	1990	1992	(1)	(1)	Not UN
USA	34	F/A-18 Hornet	Fighter aircraft	Cbt Acft	1988				..
	(500)	AGM-65B Maverick	Air-to-surface mis	M/M1	1991				..
	204	AIM-7M Sparrow	Air-to-air missile	M/M1	1988				..
	(204)	AIM-9L Sidewinder	Air-to-air missile	..	(1988)				..
	12 000	BGM-71D TOW-2	Anti-tank missile	..	(1985)	1988–92	(3 450)	(1 100)	Not UN
	3 500	FIM-92A Stinger	Portable SAM	..	1988				..
L: Germany	345	Leopard-2	Main battle tank	Tank	1983	1987–92	336	72	Not UN

Syria

	No.	Weapon designation	Weapon description		Year of order	Year(s) of deliveries	No. delivered	(No. produced)	Comments
E: Czechoslovakia	(252)	T-72	Main battle tank	Tank	1991	1992	(252)	(252)	Im: NP; Ex: Diff.
Korea, North	(8)	Scud-C launcher	Mobile SSM sys	LCA	1991				..
	(150)	Scud-C	SSM	M/M1	1989	1991–92	(80)	(40)	Im/Ex: NP
USSR	3	Kilo Class	Submarine	Ship	(1987)				..

Taiwan

	No.	Weapon designation	Weapon description		Year of order	Year(s) of deliveries	No. delivered	(No. produced)	Comments
E: France	60	Mirage-2000-5	Fighter aircraft	Cbt Acft	1992				..
	(1 000)	Magic-2	Air-to-air missile	..	1992				..
	(500)	Mica	Air-to-air missile	M/M1	(1992)				..
	6	La Fayette Class	Frigate	Ship	1991				..
Netherlands	8	DA-08	Surveillance radar	..	(1989)	1989–92	8	2	Not UN
	8	STIR	Fire control radar	..	(1989)	1989–92	8	2	Not UN
USA	(4)	E-2C Hawkeye	AEW aircraft	..	1990				..
	150	F-16A	Fighter aircraft	Cbt Acft	1992				..
	18	Model-209 AH-1W	Helicopter	Atk Helo	1992				..
	26	OH-58D Kiowa	Helicopter	Atk Helo	1991				..
	12	SH-2F Seasprite	Helicopter	Atk Helo	1992				..
	110	M-60-A3 Patton	Main battle tank	Tank	1991				..

Importer/ exporter (E) or licenser (L)	No. ordered	Weapon designation	Weapon description	UN category	Year of order/ licence	Year(s) of deliveries	No. delivered/ produced	Of which in 1992	UN Register status[b]
	8	Phalanx	CIWS	..	(1989)	1989–92	8	2	Not UN
	:	AN/MPQ-53	Fire control radar	..	(1992)				:
	3	Phalanx	CIWS	..	1992	1992	3	3	Not UN
	6	Phalanx	CIWS	:	1991				:
	3	RGM-84A launcher	ShShM launcher	M/MI	1992	1992	3	3	Not UN
	6	RIM-67A launcher	ShAM launcher	M/MI	1989				:
	8	W-160	Fire control radar	..	(1989)	1989–92	8	2	Not UN
	(144)	AGM-114A Hellfire	Anti-tank missile	..	(1991)				:
	600	AIM-7M Sparrow	Air-to-air missile	M/MI	1992				:
	900	AIM-9S Sidewinder	Air-to-air missile	.	1992				:
	(24)	RGM-84A Harpoon	ShShM	M/MI	1992	1992	(24)	(24)	Im: NP; Ex: NR
	80	RIM-67A/SM-1	ShAM	M/MI	(1989)	1989–92	(80)	(20)	Im: NP; Ex: NR
	97	RIM-67A/SM-1	ShAM	M/MI	1991				
	3	Knox Class	Frigate	Ship	1992	1992	2	2	Im: NP; Ex: NR
L: Israel	:	Gabriel-2	ShShM	M/MI	(1978)	1980–92	583	(60)	Not UN
USA	6	FFG-7	Frigate	Ship	1989				:
Thailand									
E: China	9	AS-365N Dauphin	Helicopter	..	1992				
	(450)	T-69	Main battle tank	Tank	1987	1989–92	(450)	(150)	Im: NP; Ex: NR
	4	C-801 launcher	ShShM launcher	M/MI	1988	1991–92	4	2	Not UN
	(25)	Type-311B	Fire control radar	..	1991	1991–92	(25)	(13)	Not UN
	96	C-801	ShShM	M/MI	1988	1991–92	(96)	(48)	Im: NP; Ex: PR—Diff.
	(900)	HN-5A	Portable SAM	:	1991				:
	4	Jianghu Class	Frigate	Ship	1988	1991–92	4	2	Im: NP; Ex: Conf.
	2	Naresuan Class	Frigate	Ship	1989				..

Supplier	No.	Weapon designation	Weapon description	Category	Year of order	Year(s) of deliveries	No.	No.	Comments
Czechoslovakia	36	L-39Z Albatross	Jet trainer aircraft	Cbt Acft	1992				..
France	20	Crotale NG	SAM system	..	1991				..
	(480)	VT-1	SAM	..	1991				..
Netherlands	2	STIR	Fire control radar	..	1992				..
Spain	1	ASS Bazan	Landing ship	Ship	1992				..
Switzerland	20	PC-9 Turbo Trainer	Trainer aircraft	Cbt Acft	1990	1991–92	(20)	(10)	Im: NP; Ex: NR
UK	2	Martello 743-D	Surveillance radar	..	1991	1992	(2)	(2)	Not UN
USA	38	A-7E Corsair-2	Fighter/grd attack	Cbt Acft	1991				..
	4	C-130H-30	Transport aircraft	Cbt Acft	1991				..
	18	F-16A/B	Fighter aircraft	Cbt Acft	1991				..
	25	Model 212	Helicopter	Helicopter	1990	1991–92	(23)	(12)	Not UN
	3	P-3B Orion	Maritime patrol	Cbt Acft	1989				..
	2	SH-2F Seasprite	Helicopter	Atk Helo	1989				..
	20	M-109 155mm	Self-propelled gun	LCA	(1991)	1992	(5)	(5)	Im: NP; Ex: NR
	350	M-48-A5 Patton	Main battle tank	Tank	1990				..
	300	M-60-A1 Patton	Main battle tank	Tank	1990	1991–92	(300)	(150)	Im: NP; Ex: NR
	2	Sea Sparrow VLS	ShAM launcher	..	(1991)				..
	16	AGM-84A Harpoon	Anti-ship missile	M/Ml	1990				..
	48	Sea Sparrow	ShAM	..	(1991)				..
L: UK	3	Khamronsin Class	Fast attack craft	Ship	1987	1992	3	3	Not UN
	1	Province Class	Patrol craft	..	1989	1992	1	1	Not UN
Tunisia									
E: Germany	4	Kondor Class	MCM	..	1992	1992	4	4	Not UN
Turkey									
E: France	5	Stentor	Surveillance radar	..	1987	1988–92	(5)	(1)	Not UN
	14	TRS-22XX	Surveillance radar	..	1987				..
Germany	(46)	F-4F Phantom	Fighter aircraft	Cbt Acft	(1991)	1992	46	46	Im/Ex: NR
	46	RF-4E Phantom	Recce aircraft	Cbt Acft	(1991)	1992	46	46	Im/Ex: Diff.

Importer/ exporter (E) or licenser (L)	No. ordered	Weapon designation	Weapon description	UN category	Year of order/ licence	Year(s) of deliveries	No. delivered/ produced	Of which in 1992	UN Register status[b]
	131	LARS 110mm	MRL	LCA	(1991)	1992	(50)	(50)	Im/Ex: NR
	131	M-110-A2 203mm	Self-propelled gun	LCA	(1991)				
	300	BTR-60P	APC	ACV	(1990)	1990–92	(300)	(100)	Im: NR; Ex: Conf.
	100	Leopard-1-A1	Main battle tank	Tank	(1991)	1992	15	15	Im/Ex: Diff.
	20	M-48 ARV	ARV	.	(1991)				
	10	M-48 AVLB	Bridge layer	.	(1991)	1992	(10)	(10)	Not UN
	100	Ratac-S	Battlefield radar	.	1992				:
	1	Meko-200 Type	Frigate	Ship	1990				:
	1	Meko-200 Type	Frigate	Ship	1992				:
Italy	14	SF-260D	Trainer aircraft	.	1990	1990–92	14	2	Not UN
	100	M-113	APC	ACV	(1991)				:
	4	Seaguard	Fire control radar	.	1990				:
	(48)	Aspide	ShAM	.	1990				:
Russia	17	Mi-17 Hip-H	Helicopter	.	1992	1992	(3)	(3)	Not UN
	10	BTR-60P	APC	ACV	1992	1992	10	10	Im/Ex: NR
USA	23	Model 209 AH-1S	Helicopter	Atk Helo	1990	1992	(9)	(9)	Im/Ex: Diff.
	10	R-22	Helicopter	.	1991	1992	10	10	Not UN
	45	UH-60 Blackhawk	Helicopter	.	1992	1992	5	5	Not UN
	72	M-110-A2 203mm	Self-propelled gun	LCA	(1991)				Im/Ex: PR
	300	M-113	APC	ACV	1990				Im: PR
	(250)	M-113	APC	ACV	(1991)				Im: PR
	(164)	M-60-A1 Patton	Main battle tank	Tank	(1991)				Im: Diff.; Ex: PR
	600	M-60-A3 Patton	Main battle tank	Tank	(1990)	1992	(300)	(300)	Im/Ex: Diff.
	658	M-60-A3 Patton	Main battle tank	Tank	(1991)				
	(40)	V-150 Commando	APC	ACV	1992				:
	1	AN/FPS-117	Surveillance radar	.	1991				:
	5	AN/TPQ-36	Tracking radar	.	1992				:

No.	Weapon designation	Weapon description	Code	Year of order	Year of delivery	No.	No.	Comments
2	RGM-84A launcher	ShShM launcher	M/MI	1990				..
2	Sea Sparrow launcher	ShAM launcher	..	1990				..
350	AGM-65D Maverick	Air-to-surface missile	M/MI	1991				..
100	AGM-88 Harm	Anti-radar missile	M/MI	1991				..
20	AIM-120 AMRAAM	Air-to-air missile	M/MI	(1992)				..
310	AIM-9E Sidewinder	Air-to-air missile	..	1990				..
469	FIM-92A Stinger	Portable SAM	..	1991	1992	(469)	(469)	Not UN
(48)	RGM-84A Harpoon	ShShM	M/MI	(1990)				..
L: Germany								
2	FPB-57	Fast attack craft	Ship	1991				..
1	Meko-200 Type	Frigate	Ship	1990				..
1	Meko-200 Type	Frigate	Ship	1992				..
2	Type-209/3	Submarine	Ship	1987				..
Italy 26	SF-260D	Trainer aircraft	..	1990	1992	4	4	Not UN
Spain 50	CN-235M	Transport aircraft	..	1990				..
USA 152	F-16C/D	Fighter aircraft	Cbt Acft	1984	1987–92	114	28	Not UN
40	F-16C	Fighter aircraft	Cbt Acft	1992				..
50	UH-60 Blackhawk	Helicopter	..	1992				..
120	MLRS 227mm	MRL	LCA	1988	1991–92	16	(8)	Not UN
1 698	AIFV	AIFV	ACV	1988	1990–92	311	(151)	Not UN
(4 800)	FIM-92A Stinger	Portable SAM	..	1989				..
Tuvalu								
E: Australia 1	ASI-315	Patrol craft	..	1992				..
United Arab Emirates								
E: France 500	Mistral	Portable SAM	..	1988	1991–92	(240)	(120)	Not UN
Indonesia 7	CN-235	Transport aircraft	..	1992				..
Russia 500	BMP-3	AIFV	ACV	1992	1992	(50)	(50)	Im: NP; Ex: Diff.
(4 000)	AT-10 Bastion	Anti-tank missile	..	1992	1992	(400)	(400)	Not UN
South Africa 78	G-6 155mm	Self-propelled gun	LCA	1990	1991–92	(49)	(24)	Im: NP; Ex: NR

Importer/ exporter (E) or licenser (L)	No. ordered	Weapon designation	Weapon description	UN category	Year of order/ licence	Year(s) of deliveries	No. delivered/ produced	Of which delivered in 1992	UN Register status[b]
UK	18	Hawk-100	Jet trainer aircraft	Cbt Acft	1989	1992	2	2	Im: NP; Ex: NR
USA	20	AH-64 Apache	Helicopter	Atk Helo	1991				..
	2	C-130H Hercules	Transport aircraft	..	1991				..
	620	AGM-114A Hellfire	Anti-tank missile	..	1991				..
UK									
E: USA	6	E-3D Sentry	AEW&C aircraft	..	1986	1991–92	6	3	Not UN
	1	E-3D Sentry	AEW&C aircraft	..	1987	1992	1	1	Not UN
	2	S-70C	Helicopter	..	1992				..
	210	AIM-120 AMRAAM	Air-to-air missile	M/Ml	1992				..
	220	AIM-9S Sidewinder	Air-to-air missile	..	1990	1992	(50)	(50)	Not UN
L: Brazil	128	EMB-312 Tucano	Trainer aircraft	Cbt Acft	1985	1987–92	(113)	(24)	Not UN
Switzerland	(1 000)	Piranha	APC	ACV	1991	1992	(50)	(30)	Not UN
USA	..	WS-70	Helicopter	..	1987	1987	(1)		..
	57	MLRS 227mm	MRL	LCA	1985	1989–92	(38)	(10)	Not UN
	..	BGM-71A TOW	Anti-tank missile	..	1980	1982–92	(26 201)	(2 867)	Not UN
USA									
E: Angola	250	FIM-92A Stinger	Portable SAM	..	1992	1992	250	250	Not UN
Australia	12	CH-47C Chinook	Helicopter	..	1991				..
Germany	12	MiG-23BN Flogger	Fighter/grd attack	Cbt Acft	1991	1991–92	(12)	(10)	Not UN
	48	Tpz-1 Fuchs	APC	ACV	(1991)	1991–92	28	20	Im: NR; Ex: Conf.
Italy	181	SSN-2 Styx	ShShM	M/Ml	1992	1992	181	181	Im/Ex: Conf.
	10	G-222	Transport aircraft	..	1990	1991–92	8	5	Not UN
	4	Spada battery	SAM system	..	1988				..
	16	Skyguard	Fire control radar	..	1990				..
	(144)	Aspide	SAM	..	1988				..

Supplier	No.	Weapon designation	Weapon description	Category	Year of order/licence	Year(s) of deliveries	No.	No.	Comments
Japan	(183)	Beechjet 400T	Transport aircraft	..	1990	1992	17	17	Not UN
Norway	64	Penguin-2-7	Anti-ship missile	M/MI	1990	1992	(14)	(14)	Im/Ex: NR
	82	Penguin-2-7	Anti-ship missile	M/MI	1992				..
Spain	(6)	C-212-300 Aviocar	Transport aircraft	..	1989	1990–92	(5)	(2)	Not UN
UK	38	Firefly-160	Trainer aircraft	..	1992				..
	10	Sherpa	Transport aircraft	..	1988	1990–92	(10)	(6)	Not UN
L: Israel	86	AGM-142 Have Nap	Air-to-surface mis	M/MI	1988	1989–92	(84)	(30)	Not UN; Im/Ex: PR—Diff.
Italy	17	Osprey Class	MCM	..	1986	1992	(1)	(1)	Not UN
Switzerland	..	ADATS LOS-FH	SAM	..	1987	1991–92	(198)	(100)	Not UN
UK	302	T-45 Hawk	Jet trainer aircraft	Cbt Acft	1986	1988–92	(15)	(13)	Not UN
	436	M-119 105mm	Towed gun	LCA	1987	1990–92	(106)	(50)	Not UN
	13	Cyclone Class	Patrol craft	..	1990	1992	(4)	(4)	Not UN
Uruguay									
E: Switzerland	6	PC-7 Turbo Trainer	Trainer aircraft	Cbt Acft	1992	1992	6	6	Im/Ex: NR
UK	2	Wessex	Helicopter	..	1992	1992	2	1	Not UN
Venezuela									
E: Brazil	100	EE-11 Urutu	APC	ACV	1988	1989–92	(40)	(10)	Ex: NR
France	18	Mirage-50EV	Fighter	Cbt Acft	1988	1991–92	(16)	(8)	Im: NP; Ex: Diff.
	(50)	AM-39 Exocet	Anti-ship missile	M/MI	(1988)				..
	(100)	Magic-2	Air-to-air missile	..	1988	1991–92	(40)	(20)	Not UN
Spain	2	C-212-300 Aviocar	Transport aircraft	..	(1991)				..
USA	18	OV-10E Bronco	Close support ac	Cbt Acft	1991				..
	(6)	RGM-84A launcher	ShShM launcher	M/MI	1989				..
	18	RGM-84A Harpoon	ShShM	M/MI	1989				..
Zaire									
E: France	13	AMX-13	Light tank	Tank	1989				..

Importer/ exporter (E) or licenser (L)	No. ordered	Weapon designation	Weapon description	UN category	Year of order/ licence	Year(s) of deliveries	No. delivered/ produced	Of which delivered in 1992	UN Register status[b]
Zimbabwe									
E: UK	5	Hawk	Jet trainer aircraft	Cbt Acft	1990	1991–92	(5)	(2)	Im: NP; Ex: Diff.

[a] The SIPRI register lists major weapons on order or under delivery, or for which the licence was bought and production was under way or completed during 1992. 'Year(s) of deliveries' includes aggregates of all deliveries and licensed production since the beginning of the contract. Entries are alphabetical, by importer, exporter and licenser. Abbreviations, acronyms and conventions are explained on pages xi–xii. The sources and methods for data in the SIPRI register are explained in *SIPRI Yearbook 1993* (Oxford University Press: Oxford, 1993), appendix 10D, pp. 519–20. This register is adapted from the register that appears in the *SIPRI Yearbook 1993*, appendix 10C, pp. 483–518. The changes made here appear in the final column of the *Yearbook* register, 'Comments', where the *SIPRI Yearbook 1993* gives information about the conditions and content of contracts, where available; for the purpose of comparing the SIPRI register with the UN Register, these comments are not necessary. In addition, three columns have been added for the comparison of the registers: 'UN category', denotes, if applicable, the category under which the weapon should fall in the UN Register definitions. 'Of which in 1992' gives the number of items delivered in the calendar year 1992. 'UN Register status' gives the evaluation of the comparison between the SIPRI register and the data in the UN Register for arms exports and imports in 1992.

[b] Abbreviations in column for UN Register status:

Im   Importer

Ex   Exporter

NR   Not reported to the UN Register

NP   Non-participation

NV   Not verifiable because of a lack of a precise description of the equipment in the return to the UN Register

Conf.   Confirming the transfer: the entry in the SIPRI register is the same or similar to the entry in the UN Register

Diff.   Different from SIPRI: the transfer or order is reported in the SIPRI register and in the UN Register, but the number of items, exact designation and/or delivery years are different, or it is considered licensed production by SIPRI

Not UN Item does not require reporting to the UN Register

PR   Probably reported: a transfer is reported in the SIPRI register and to the UN Register, but there is uncertainty regarding whether both report the same deal and/or whether it is the same weapon designation

PR—Diff. Probably reported, but when it has been, delivery year and/or numbers differ from those reported by SIPRI

Annexe 3. Documentation

REPORT OF THE UNITED NATIONS SECRETARY-GENERAL ON THE REGISTER OF CONVENTIONAL ARMS

. . .

INTRODUCTION

1. On 9 December 1991, as part of the larger family of international efforts to promote transparency in military matters, the United Nations General Assembly adopted resolution 46/36 L entitled "Transparency in armaments" (for the text of the resolution, see appendix A). That resolution established the Register of Conventional Arms to include data on international arms transfers as well as available background information provided by Member States on military holdings, procurement through national production and relevant policies. The Secretary-General's action to that effect was communicated to all Member States in a note verbale of 1 January 1992. In accordance with that resolution Member States are requested to provide data on an annual basis by 30 April each year in respect of imports into and exports from their territory in the previous calendar year, with the first such registration to take place by 30 April 1993 in respect of the calendar year 1992.

2. In paragraph 8 of the same resolution, the Assembly:

"*Also requests* the Secretary-General, with the assistance of a panel of governmental technical experts to be nominated by him on the basis of equitable geographical representation, to elaborate the technical procedures and to make any adjustments to the annex to the present resolution necessary for the effective operation of the Register, and to prepare a report on the modalities for early expansion of the scope of the Register by the addition of further categories of equipment and inclusion of data on military holdings and procurement through national production, and to report to the General Assembly at its forty-seventh session."

3. In paragraph 11 (*a*) of the same resolution, the Assembly invites Member States to provide the Secretary-General, not later than 30 April 1994, with their views on the "operation of the Register during its first two years" and "the addition of further categories of equipment and the elaboration of the Register to include military holdings and procurement through national production". In addition, in paragraph 11 (*b*) of the resolution, the Assembly requests the Secretary-General, "with the assistance of a group of governmental experts convened in 1994 on the basis of equitable geographical representation, to prepare a report on the continuing operation of the Register and its further development, taking into account the work of the Conference on Disarmament, as set forth in paragraphs 12 to 15 below, and the views expressed by Member States for submission to the General Assembly with a view to a decision at its forty-ninth session".

4. In paragraph 12 of the same resolution, the Assembly:

"*Requests* the Conference on Disarmament to address, as soon as possible, the question of the interrelated aspects of the excessive and destabilizing accumulation of arms, including military holdings and procurement through national production, and to elaborate universal and non-discriminatory practical means to increase openness and transparency in this field."

In paragraph 13 of the resolution, the Assembly also requested the Conference on Disarmament, *inter alia,* to elaborate practical means to increase openness and transparency "related to the transfer of high technology with military applications and to weapons of mass destruction, in accordance with existing legal instruments".

5. Also, in paragraph 14 of the same resolution, the Assembly

"*Invites* the Secretary-General to provide to the Conference on Disarmament all relevant information, including, *inter alia*, views submitted to him by Member States and information provided under the United Nations system for the standardized reporting of military expenditures, as well as the work of the United Nations Disarmament Commission under its agenda item entitled 'Objective information on military matters'."

In paragraph 15 of the resolution, the Assembly "*Further requests* the Conference on Disarmament to include in its annual report to the General Assembly a report on its work on this issue".

6. In addition to the work of the Conference on Disarmament, Member States, in paragraphs 16 and 17 of the resolution, are urged to take measures at the national, regional and subregional levels aimed at increased openness and transparency in armaments.

7. The present report, a step in the implementation of General Assembly resolution 46/36 L, is the result of the work of the Panel of Governmental Technical Experts.

I. TECHNICAL PROCEDURES FOR THE OPERATION OF THE REGISTER

A. *General*

8. Part I of the work of the Panel stems from the mandate contained in paragraph 8 of General Assembly resolution 46/36 L, namely "to elaborate the technical procedures and to make any adjustments to the annex to the present resolution necessary for the effective operation of the Register". It is further based on paragraph 7 of the resolution, in which the Assembly requests the Secretary-General to establish and maintain the Register "in accordance with procedures and input requirements initially comprising those set out in the annex to the present resolution and subsequently incorporating any adjustment to the annex decided upon by the General Assembly at the forty-seventh session in the light of the recommendations of the panel referred to in paragraph 8".

B. *Arms transfers*

9. Paragraph 2 (a) of the annex to General Assembly resolution 46/36 L states that "Member States are requested to provide data for the Register, addressed to the Secretary-General, on the number of items in the following categories of equipment imported into or exported from their territory". The Panel did not attempt to define arms transfers but, for the purpose of the Register, considered that the terms "imported into or exported from their territory" needed some clarification, as stated in paragraphs 12 and 13 below.

10. International arms transfers involve, in addition to the physical movement of equipment into or from national territory, the transfer of title to and control over the equipment.

11. An international arms transfer may also occur without the movement of equipment across State frontiers if a State, or its agent, is granted title and control over the equipment in the territory of the supplier State. Therefore, a transfer of arms to a State would occur when its forces stationed abroad are granted title and control of equipment by the host country or any third State, or when title and control of such equipment are transferred to the host country or any third State. Additionally, if title and con-

trol of equipment temporarily stored or prepositioned on the territory of another State are granted to the host country by the owner, then an international transfer has occurred.

12. Since the supply of equipment by a State to units of its armed forces stationed abroad does not involve transfer of national title and control, such supply is not considered an international transfer. Equipment of a State can be temporarily stored or prepositioned on the territory of another State with no transfer of title and control of this equipment. This is not considered an international arms transfer.

13. In paragraphs 2 (c) and (d) of the annex to the same resolution, Member States are "requested to provide data on an annual basis by 30 April each year in respect of imports into and exports from their territory in the previous calendar year", with the first such registration taking place by 30 April 1993 in respect of the calendar year 1992. To be reported are those transfers considered by States to have been effected during the relevant reporting year, in conformity with their respective national criteria used to define when a transfer becomes effective. Member States are invited to indicate such national criteria with their return.

C. *Categories of equipment the transfers of which are to be registered*

14. Paragraph 2 (a) of the annex to General Assembly resolution 46/36 L also identifies the following seven categories of equipment on which Member States are requested to supply data to the Register—battle tanks, armoured combat vehicles, large calibre artillery systems, combat aircraft, attack helicopters, warships, and missiles or missile systems. Based on the adjustments to the annex developed by the Panel pursuant to its mandate, the categories and their definitions to be used for reporting to the Register are, as follows:

I. *Battle tanks*

Tracked or wheeled self-propelled armoured fighting vehicles with high cross-country mobility and a high level of self-protection, weighing at least 16.5 metric tonnes unladen weight, with a high muzzle velocity direct fire main gun of at least 75 millimetres calibre.

II. *Armoured combat vehicles*

Tracked, semi-tracked or wheeled self-propelled vehicles, with armoured protection and cross-country capability, either: (a) designed and equipped to transport a squad of four or more infantrymen, or (b) armed with an integral or organic weapons of at least 12.5 millimetres calibre or a missile launcher.

III. *Large calibre artillery systems*

Guns, howitzers, artillery pieces, combining the characteristics of a gun or a howitzer, mortars or multiple-launch rocket systems, capable of engaging surface targets by delivering primarily indirect fire, with a calibre of 100 milli metres and above.

IV. *Combat aircraft*

Fixed-wing or variable-geometry wing aircraft designed, equipped or modified to engage targets by employing guided missiles, unguided rockets, bombs, guns, cannons, or other weapons of destruction, including versions of these aircraft which perform specialized electronic warfare, suppression of air defence or reconnaissance missions. The term "combat aircraft" does not include primary trainer aircraft, unless designed, equipped or modified as described above.

V. *Attack helicopters*

Rotary-wing aircraft designed, equipped or modified to engage tar-

gets by employing guided or unguided anti-armour, air-to-surface,
air-to-subsurface, or air-to-air
weapons and equipped with an integrated fire control and aiming
system for these weapons, including versions of these aircraft which
perform specialized reconnaissance
or electronic warfare missions.

VI. *Warships*

Vessels or submarines armed and
equipped for military use with a
standard displacement of 750
metric tonnes or above, and those
with a standard displacement of
less than 750 metric tonnes,
equipped for launching missiles
with a range of at least 25 kilometers or torpedoes with similar
range.

VII. *Missiles and missile launchers*

Guided or unguided rockets, ballistic or cruise missiles capable of delivering a warhead or weapon of
destruction to a range of at least 25
kilometers, and means designed or
modified specifically for launching
such missiles or rockets, if not
covered by categories I through VI.
For the purpose of the Register,
this category:
(a) Also includes remotely-piloted
vehicles with the characteristics
for missiles as defined above;
(b) Does not include ground-to-air
missiles.

D. *Standardized form for reporting international transfers*

15. In paragraph 9 of General Assembly resolution 46/36 L, the Assembly
"calls upon all Member States to provide annually for the Register data on
imports and exports of arms". Also, in
the fourteenth preambular paragraph of
the resolution, the Assembly refers to the
utility of "the standardized reporting of
international arms transfers" for the
promotion of transparency in military
matters. Pursuant to its mandate, the
Panel developed the standardized reporting form (see appendix B to the
present report) to be used by Member
States when providing data for the
Register on the number of items
exported and imported in each of the
seven categories of equipment defined in
paragraph 14 above.

16. Pending the review of the operation of the Register in 1994, data on
missiles and missile launchers are to be
submitted as a single entry in terms of an
aggregate number:
(a) For missiles associated with other
launchers covered under categories I to
VI, the number 606 will be entered. If,
in a given year, a country exports to a
specific country 50 missiles of one type
and 80 of another type, the number 130
will be entered in column B.
(b) Missiles that are launched from
equipment in categories I to VI will be
reported in category VII. Missile
launchers integral to equipment in categories I to VI are considered a component of that equipment and are not to be
reported in category VII missile launchers. For example, air-to-air missiles for
combat aircraft are reported in category VII, but the missile launcher is
considered to be the aircraft and its
transfer is to be reported in category IV.

17. Column A in the form lists the
seven categories as defined above. In
column B the exporter State(s) (in the
import form) and the importer State(s)
(in the export form) are to be entered. In
addition, column B includes a serial
number, identifying the different exporter and importer State(s) as appropriate. Column C in the form includes
the number of items of equipment the
transfer of which was effected during the
relevant reporting year. Transfers, as described in paragraphs 12 and 13 to be reported, are those that have been effected
during the relevant reporting year.

18. Columns D and E on the form are
included to accommodate data on countries which are not the countries of ex-

port or import. In the case of an international transfer involving an export of equipment by a State other than the State of origin, the name of the country of origin should be entered in column D. In the case of an international arms transfer involving transport of equipment to an intermediate location, or involving retention of equipment at an intermediate location for the purpose of the integration of equipment of one category within the Register with equipment of another category, the name of the intermediate location should be entered in column E (e.g. the export of missiles to an intermediate location for integration there with a combat aircraft manufactured at the intermediate location, or vice versa).

19. The right hand column on the form, divided into two parts, "description of item" and "comments on the transfer", is designed to accommodate additional information on the transfers. Since the provision of such information might be affected by security and other relevant concerns of Member States, this column should be filled in at Member States" discretion; no specific patterns are prescribed. To aid the understanding of the international transfers reported, Member States may wish to enter designation, type or model of equipment, or use various descriptive elements contained in the definitions of categories I to VII, which also serve as guides to describe equipment transferred. Member States may also use this column to clarify, for example, that a transfer is of obsolete equipment, the result of co-production, or for other such explanatory remarks as Member States see fit.

E. *Available background information regarding military holdings, procurement through national production and relevant policies*

20. Pursuant to paragraph 7 of General Assembly resolution 46/36 L, the Register is to include "information provided by Member States on military holdings, procurement through national production and relevant policies". Pursuant to paragraph 3 (*a*) of the annex to that resolution, "Member States are invited also to provide to the Secretary-General available background information regarding their military holdings, procurement through national production, and relevant policies".

21. The reporting of this information is voluntary and Member States may submit this information in any form they wish.

F. *Operation of the Register*

1. *Submission of data on transfers*

22. According to paragraph 2 (*c*) of the annex to General Assembly resolution 46/36 L, "each Member State is requested to provide data on an annual basis by 30 April each year in respect of imports into and exports from their territory in the previous calendar year". Paragraph 2 (d) of the annex to the resolution states that "the first such registration shall take place by 30 April 1993 in respect of the calendar year 1992".

23. Data should be submitted on the form (see appendix B below) taking account of the present report, by 30 April annually to United Nations Headquarters in New York.

24. Member States that do not have anything to report should file a "nil report", clearly stating that no exports or imports have taken place in any of the seven categories during the reporting period.

25. The Office for Disarmament Affairs in the United Nations Secretariat should receive and compile for the Secretary-General's annual report data sheets submitted by Member States and establish a computerized database which will store the reported data.

2. *Submission of available background information*

26. Available background information to be included in the index (as envisaged

in paragraph 5 of the annex to General Assembly resolution 46/36 L) of the annual report of the Secretary-General should be submitted by 30 April of each year.

27. The Office for Disarmament Affairs will maintain in its computerized database a running index of the background information submitted, by country, date and title. Member States should assign titles to their submissions.

G. *Annual consolidated report by the Secretary-General*

28. According to paragraph 5 of the annex to General Assembly resolution 46/36 L, "the Secretary-General shall provide annually a consolidated report to the General Assembly of the data registered, together with an index of the other interrelated information".

29. Section I of the annual report will be a compilation of the reports submitted by Member States on the standardized reporting form (see appendix B below), as they are received by the Secretary-General.

30. Section II of the report will be an index of the background information submitted by Member States.

H. *Access to the Register*

31. According to paragraph 4 of the annex to General Assembly resolution 46/36 L, "the Register shall be open for consultation by representatives of Member States at any time". The Office for Disarmament Affairs should therefore make available the data and information received to any requesting Member State.

32. Member States should have access to the computerized data contained in the Register of Conventional Arms, either on-line (electronically) or by physical transfer of disks.

33. As well as the Secretary-General's consolidated annual report to the United Nations General Assembly, it is recommended that the available background information submitted by Member States

be open to the public.

II. MODALITIES FOR EARLY EXPANSION OF THE SCOPE OF THE REGISTER

A. *General*

34. In paragraph 8 of General Assembly resolution 46/36 L, the Assembly requests the Secretary-General to prepare, with the assistance of a panel of governmental technical experts, "a report on the modalities for early expansion of the scope of the Register by the addition of further categories of equipment and inclusion of data on military holdings and procurement through national production and to report to the General Assembly at its forty-seventh session".

35. According to paragraph 11 (*a*) of the same resolution, the Assembly "*invites* Member States to provide the Secretary-General with their views on: (i) the operation of the Register during its first two years; (ii) the addition of further categories of equipment and the elaboration of the Register to include military holdings and procurement through national production". In paragraph 11 (*b*) of the resolution, the Assembly

"*Requests* the Secretary-General, with the assistance of a group of governmental experts convened in 1994 on the basis of equitable geographical representation, to prepare a report on the continuing operation of the Register and its further development."

In addition, in paragraph 12 of the resolution, the Assembly

"*Requests* the Conference on Disarmament to address, as soon as possible, the question of the interrelated aspects of the excessive and destabilizing accumulation of arms, including military holdings and procurement through national production, and to elaborate universal and non-discriminatory practical means to increase openness and transparency in this field."

In paragraph 13 of the resolution, the

Assembly "*also requests* the Conference on Disarmament to address the problem of, and the elaboration of practical means to increase, openness and transparency related to the transfer of high technology with military applications and to weapons of mass destruction, in accordance with existing legal instruments".

36. The issues identified below are offered as a first step in the consideration of modalities for expansion of the Register. The future development of the Register should take into consideration other efforts designed to enhance transparency in armaments and thus contribute to the enhancement of confidence among States.

B. *Review of the operation of the Register*

37. Since the group of governmental experts to be convened in 1994 is requested in paragraph 11 (b) of the resolution to "prepare a report on the continuing operation of the Register and its further development", it should assess the first two years of the operation of the Register addressing, *inter alia*, the following:

(a) The description of international arms transfers as contained in paragraphs 12 and 13 of the present report;

(b) The standardized reporting form as contained in appendix B to the present report;

(c) The extent of participation by Member States in the Register.

C. *Modalities for the addition of further categories of equipment*

38. To assist in the future deliberations on the addition of further categories of equipment, the Panel felt that the following might be taken into account:

(a) The possibility of expanding the existing categories by modifying their existing parameters (e.g. tonnage, range, calibre, roles, capabilities and characteristics); or by introducing new parameters or by including subcategories;

(b) The possibility of including new categories:

(i) To take account of significant technical developments relating to the weapons within the existing categories;

(ii) To include weapons not covered by existing categories which should be considered because of their destabilizing potential. In addition to the points above, future deliberations should draw upon the experience of the operation of the Register.

39. While no decisions are required to be taken regarding the expansion of the scope of the Register until 1994, the Panel considered the possibility of additional categories of equipment that could be reported. It was considered that possible additional categories should be based on substantial agreement so as to ensure the widest possible participation in the Register. A key principle for adding categories should be that of military relevance in terms of the significance of their impact on regional and global stability. The objective should be to enhance transparency, without prejudice to the security of Member States, and help avoid destabilizing accumulations of arms.

40. In the Panel's discussions of the scope of certain categories of equipment, as defined in part I of the present report, issues were raised which, without prejudice to how the forums concerned organize their work, are listed below for their benefit:

(a) Aerial refuelling aircraft;

(b) Reconnaissance aircraft (fixed and rotary wing);

(c) Airborne electronic warfare equipment (fixed and rotary wing);

(d) Airborne early warning and command and control systems (fixed and rotary wing);

(e) Warships: the possibility of lowering or removing the tonnage threshold;

(f) Missiles:

(i) Ground to air missiles;

(ii) Range of missiles;

(iii) Unmanned air-breathing vehicles;

(iv) Close-in anti-missile defence system;

(v) Disaggregation of missiles and launchers for the purpose of reporting;

(g) Ammunition, *inter alia*:

(i) Precision-guided;

(ii) Cluster bombs;

(iii) Fuel-air explosives;

(iv) Remotely delivered mines;

(h) Systems for the delivery of weapons of mass destruction not already covered by the Register.

D. *Modalities for inclusion of data on military holdings and procurement through national production*

41. To assist in the future deliberations on the subject of including data on military holdings and procurement through national production in the Register, the Panel felt that a common understanding is required of what constitutes military holdings and procurement through national production. The terms military holdings and procurement through national production need to be defined for the purpose of the Register. With these considerations in mind the following questions were raised by the Panel:

(a) What constitutes armed forces for the purpose of reporting military holdings? In addition to holdings of regular forces, are those of paramilitary, coastguard, reserve and other types of forces, such as organizations designed and structured to perform peacetime internal security functions, to be included?

(b) Should a legal approach be adopted, defining armed forces as those which take on combatant status in time of war?

(c) Should military holdings be reported on the basis of the same categories of equipment as for arms transfers?

(d) Should equipment in storage or mothballed, awaiting decommissioning or in transit be considered as military holdings and be included?

(e) Should equipment in the process of manufacture or manufacturing-related testing, used exclusively for research and development or belonging to historical collections be included?

(f) Regarding data on procurement through national production:

(i) Should data be reported in values and/or in the number of items procured?

(ii) Should procurement be regarded as procurement from any national production facility, whatever the arrangement may be, for example, international collaborative production, licence, and so forth?

(iii) Should equipment procured externally in separate parts and later assembled be considered procurement through national production or reported as imported equipment?

(iv) Should data on procurement through national production relate to equipment ordered by or only that actually delivered to the armed forces (however defined)?

(v) Should data on the upgrading of equipment be included?

III. RESOURCE IMPLICATIONS FOR THE MAINTENANCE OF THE REGISTER

42. At the Panel's request, the following estimates of resources required for the operation of the Register were provided by the United Nations Secretariat.

43. As currently envisaged, the initial operation and storage of the data of the Register can be accommodated through the projected hardware and software system within the Office for Disarmament Affairs. Incremental start-up costs would be limited to computer hardware and software required for system development, and testing at an estimated cost of $50,000.

44. However, the subsequent operation of the system, that is, installation of

the data concerning arms transfers, as well as "background information regarding military holdings, procurement through national production and relevant policies", as Member States were invited to do so by the resolution, will considerably increase the operational complexity of the system and the workload of the Secretariat.

45. Moreover, for the database of the Register to be electronically accessible by Member States, an initial estimated amount of $75,000 would be required to develop the system, support it and distribute related instructional and training material.

46. The development, upgrading and maintenance of the Register would require staff from the Office for Disarmament Affairs with politico-military expertise, especially in the area of arms transfers, in combination with a highly specialized knowledge in the field of database management and systems analysis. Such expertise is currently not available within the Office for Disarmament Affairs. In addition, the day today operation of the Register requires one General Service staff experienced in the basics of programming.

47. Based on available information as well as the experience gained in the maintenance of the United Nations system for the standardized reporting of military expenditures, it is estimated that the Office for Disarmament Affairs would require three additional posts at a total cost of $228,000 per year. The breakdown is divided as follows: one post at the P-5 level—$115,700; one post at the P-2 level—$67,500; and one post at the G-5 level—$45,400 per annum.

48. These estimates are approximations, since it would be impossible to forecast accurately the volume of the work involved in the operation of the Register.

49. The Panel of Governmental Technical Experts recommends that the issue be reviewed by the appropriate United Nations bodies to ensure the most cost-effective use of resources.

APPENDIX A

General Assembly resolution 46/36 L of 9 December 1991

Transparency in armaments

The General Assembly,

Realizing that excessive and destabilizing arms build-ups pose a threat to national, regional and international peace and security, particularly by aggravating tensions and conflict situations, giving rise to serious and urgent concerns,

Noting with satisfaction that the current international environment and recent agreements and measures in the field of arms limitation and disarmament make it a propitious time to work towards easing tensions and a just resolution of conflict situations, as well as more openness and transparency in military matters,

Recalling the consensus among Member States on implementing confidence-building measures, including transparency and exchange of relevant information on armaments, likely to reduce the occurrence of dangerous misperceptions about the intentions of States and to promote trust among States,

Considering that increased openness and transparency in the field of armaments could enhance confidence, ease tensions, strengthen regional and international peace and security and contribute to restraint in military production and the transfer of arms,

Realizing the urgent need to resolve underlying conflicts, to diminish tensions and to accelerate efforts towards general and complete disarmament under strict and effective international control with a view to maintaining regional and international peace and security in a world free from the scourge of war and the burden of armaments,

Recalling also that in paragraph 85 of the Final Document of the Tenth Special Session of the General Assembly it urged major arms supplier and recipient countries to consult on the limitation of all types of international transfer of conventional arms,

Disturbed by the destabilizing and destructive effects of the illicit arms trade, particularly for the internal situation of affected States and the violation of human rights,

Bearing in mind that, in accordance with the Charter of the United Nations, Member States have undertaken to promote the establishment and maintenance of international peace and security with the least diversion for armaments of the world's human and economic resources, and that the reduction of world military expenditures could have a significant positive impact for the social and economic development of all peoples,

Reaffirming the important role of the United Nations in the field of disarmament and the commitment of Member States to take concrete steps in order to strengthen that role,

Recalling its resolution 43/75 I of 7 December 1988,

Welcoming the study submitted by the Secretary-General, pursuant to paragraph 5 of resolution 43/75 I and prepared with the assistance of governmental experts, on ways and means of promoting transparency in international transfers of conventional arms, as well as the problem of the illicit arms trade, taking into account views of Member States and other relevant information,

Recognizing the major contribution of an enhanced level of transparency in armaments to confidence-building and security among States, and also recognizing the urgent need to establish, under the auspices of the United Nations, as a first step in this direction, a universal and non-discriminatory register to include data on international arms transfers as well as other interrelated information provided to the Secretary-General,

Stressing the importance of greater transparency in the interest of promoting readiness to exercise restraint in accumulation of armaments,

Considering that the standardized reporting of international arms transfers together with the provision of other interrelated information to a United Nations register will constitute further important steps forward in the promotion of transparency in military matters and, as such, will enhance the role and effectiveness of the United Nations in promoting arms limitation and disarmament, as well as in maintaining international peace and security;

Recognizing also the importance of the prevention of the proliferation of nuclear weapons and other weapons of mass destruction,

1. *Recognizes* that an increased level of openness and transparency in the field of armaments would enhance confidence, promote stability, help States to exercise restraint, ease tensions and strengthen regional and international peace and security;

2. *Declares its determination* to prevent the excessive and destabilizing accumulation of arms, including conventional arms, in order to promote stability and strengthen regional or international peace and security, taking into account the legitimate security needs of States and the principle of undiminished security at the lowest possible level of armaments;

3. *Reaffirms* the inherent right to individual or collective self-defence recognized in Article 51 of the Charter of the United Nations, which implies that States also have the right to acquire arms with which to defend themselves;

4. *Reiterates its conviction*, as expressed in its resolution 43/75 I, that arms transfers in all their aspects deserve serious consideration by the international community, *inter alia*, because of:

(a) Their potential effects in further

destabilizing areas where tension and regional conflict threaten international peace and security and national security;

(b) Their potentially negative effects on the progress of the peaceful social and economic development of all peoples;

(c) The danger of increasing illicit and covert arms trafficking;

5. *Calls upon* all Member States to exercise due restraint in exports and imports of conventional arms, particularly in situations of tension or conflict, and to ensure that they have in place an adequate body of laws and administrative procedures regarding the transfer of arms and to adopt strict measures for their enforcement;

6. *Expresses its appreciation to* the Secretary-General for his study on ways and means of promoting transparency in international transfers of conventional arms, which also addressed the problem of the illicit arms trade;

7. *Requests* the Secretary-General to establish and maintain at United Nations Headquarters in New York a universal and non-discriminatory Register of Conventional Arms, to include data on international arms transfers as well as information provided by Member States on military holdings, procurement through national production and relevant policies, as set out in paragraph 10 below and in accordance with procedures and input requirements initially comprising those set out in the annex to the present resolution and subsequently incorporating any adjustments to the annex decided upon by the General Assembly at its forty-seventh session in the light of the recommendations of the panel referred to in paragraph 8 below;

8. *Also requests* the Secretary-General, with the assistance of a panel of governmental technical experts to be nominated by him on the basis of equitable geographical representation, to elaborate the technical procedures and to make any adjustments to the annex to

the present resolution necessary for the effective operation of the Register, and to prepare a report on the modalities for early expansion of the scope of the Register by the addition of further categories of equipment and inclusion of data on military holdings and procurement through national production, and to report to the General Assembly at its forty-seventh session;

9. *Calls upon* all Member States to provide annually for the Register data on imports and exports of arms in accordance with the procedures established by paragraphs 7 and 8 above;

10. *Invites* Member States, pending the expansion of the Register, also to provide to the Secretary-General, with their annual report on imports and exports of arms, available background information regarding their military holdings, procurement through national production and relevant policies, and requests the Secretary-General to record this material and to make it available for consultation by Member States at their request;

11. *Decides*, with a view to future expansion, to keep the scope of and the participation in the Register under review, and, to this end:

(a) *Invites* Member States to provide the Secretary-General with their views, not later than 30 April 1994, on:

(i) The operation of the Register during its first two years;

(ii) The addition of further categories of equipment and the elaboration of the Register to include military holdings and procurement through national production;

(b) *Requests* the Secretary-General, with the assistance of a group of governmental experts convened in 1994 on the basis of equitable geographical representation, to prepare a report on the continuing operation of the Register and its further development, taking into account the work of the Conference on Disarmament as set forth in paragraphs 12 to 15 below and the views expressed by Member States, for submission to the General Assembly with a view to a decision at its forty-ninth session;

12. *Requests* the Conference on Disarmament to address, as soon as possible, the question of the interrelated aspects of the excessive and destabilizing accumulation of arms, including military holdings and procurement through national production, and to elaborate universal and non-discriminatory practical means to increase openness and transparency in this field;

13. *Also requests* the Conference on Disarmament to address the problems of, and the elaboration of practical means to increase, openness and transparency related to the transfer of high technology with military applications and to weapons of mass destruction, in accordance with existing legal instruments;

14. *Invites* the Secretary-General to provide to the Conference on Disarmament all relevant information, including, *inter alia*, views submitted to him by Member States and information provided under the United Nations system for the standardized reporting of military expenditures, as well as on the work of the Disarmament Commission under its agenda item entitled "Objective information on military matters";

15. *Further requests* the Conference on Disarmament to include in its annual report to the General Assembly a report on its work on this issue;

16. *Invites* all Member States, in the meantime, to take measures on a national, regional and global basis, including within the appropriate forums, to promote openness and transparency in armaments;

17. *Calls upon* all Member States to cooperate at a regional and subregional level, taking fully into account the specific conditions prevailing in the region or subregion, with a view to enhancing and coordinating international efforts aimed at increased openness and transparency in armaments;

18. *Also invites* all Member States to inform the Secretary-General of their national arms import and export policies, legislation and administrative procedures, both as regards authorization of arms transfers and prevention of illicit transfers;

19. *Requests* the Secretary-General to report to the General Assembly at its forty-seventh session on progress made in implementing the present resolution, including relevant information provided by Member States;

20. *Notes* that effective implementation of the present resolution will require an up-to-date database system in the Department for Disarmament Affairs of the Secretariat;

21. *Decides* to include in the provisional agenda of its forty-seventh session an item entitled "Transparency in armaments".

ANNEX

Register of Conventional Arms

1. The Register of Conventional Arms ("the Register") shall be established, with effect from 1 January 1992, and maintained at the Headquarters of the United Nations in New York.

2. Concerning international arms transfers:

(a) Member States are requested to provide data for the Register, addressed to the Secretary-General, on the number of items in the following categories of equipment imported into or exported from their territory:

I. *Battle tanks*

A tracked or wheeled self-propelled armoured fighting vehicle with high cross-country mobility and a high level of self-protection, weighing at least 16.5 metric tonnes unladen weight, with a high muzzle velocity direct fire main gun of at least 75 millimetres calibre.

II. *Armoured combat vehicles*

A tracked or wheeled self-propelled vehicle, with armoured protection and cross-country capability, either: (*a*) designed and equipped to transport a squad of four or more infantrymen, or (b) armed with an integral or organic weapon of at least 20 millimetres calibre or an anti-tank missile launcher.

III. *Large calibre artillery systems*

A gun, howitzer, artillery piece combining the characteristics of a gun and a howitzer, mortar or multiple-launch rocket system, capable of engaging surface targets by delivering primarily indirect fire, with a calibre of 100 millimetres and above.

IV. *Combat aircraft*

A fixed-wing or variable-geometry wing aircraft armed and equipped to engage targets by employing guided missiles, unguided rockets, bombs, guns, cannons, or other weapons of destruction.

V. *Attack helicopters*

A rotary-wing aircraft equipped to employ anti-armour, air-to-ground, or air-to-air guided weapons and equipped with an integrated fire control and aiming system for these weapons.

VI. *Warships*

A vessel or submarine with a standard displacement of 850 metric tonnes or above, armed or equipped for military use.

VII. *Missiles or missile systems*

A guided rocket, ballistic or cruise missile capable of delivering a payload to a range of at least 25 kilometres, or a vehicle, apparatus or device designed or modified for launching such munitions.

(*b*) Data on imports provided under the present paragraph shall also specify the supplying State; data on exports shall also specify the recipient State and the State of origin if not the exporting State;

(*c*) Each Member State is requested to provide data on an annual basis by 30 April each year in respect of imports into and exports from their territory in the previous calendar year;

(*d*) The first such registration shall take place by 30 April 1993 in respect of the calendar year 1992;

(*e*) The data so provided shall be recorded in respect of each Member State;

(*f*) Arms "exports and imports" represent in the present resolution, including its annex, all forms of arms transfers under terms of grant, credit, barter or cash.

3. Concerning other interrelated information:

(*a*) Member States are invited also to provide to the Secretary-General available background information regarding their military holdings, procurement through national production, and relevant policies;

(*b*) The information so provided shall be recorded in respect of each Member State.

4. The Register shall be open for consultation by representatives of Member States at any time.

5. In addition, the Secretary-General shall provide annually a consolidated report to the General Assembly of the data registered, together with an index of the other interrelated information.

APPENDIX B
Standardized forms for reporting international transfers of conventional arms

EXPORTS
Report of international conventional arms transfers
(according to United Nations General Assembly resolution 46/36 L)
Reporting country: _____
Calendar year: 1992

A	B	C	D*	E*	REMARKS**	
Category (I–VII)	Final importer State(s)	Number of items	State of origin (if not exporter)	Intermediate location (if any)	Description of item	Comments on the transfer
I. Battle tanks 1) 2) 3)						
II. Armoured combat vehicles 1) 2) 3)						
III. Large calibre artillery systems 1) 2) 3)						
IV. Combat aircraft 1) 2) 3)						
V. Attack helicopters 1) 2) 3)						
VI. Warships 1) 2) 3)						
VII. Missiles and missile launchers 1) 2) 3)						

Background information provided: yes/no

* See para. 18 of the present report.
** See para. 19 of the present report.

APPENDIX B (concluded)
Standardized forms for reporting international transfers of conventional arms

IMPORTS
Report of international conventional arms transfers
(according to United Nations General Assembly resolution 46/36 L)
Reporting country: _____
Calendar year: 1992

A	B	C	D*	E*	REMARKS**	
Category (I–VII)	Final exporter State(s)	Number of items	State of origin (if not exporter)	Intermediate location (if any)	Description of item	Comments on the transfer
I. Battle tanks 1) 2) 3)						
II. Armoured combat vehicles 1) 2) 3)						
III. Large calibre artillery systems 1) 2) 3)						
IV. Combat aircraft 1) 2) 3)						
V. Attack helicopters 1) 2) 3)						
VI. Warships 1) 2) 3)						
VII. Missiles and missile launchers 1) 2) 3)						

Background information provided: yes/no

* See para. 18 of the present report.
** See para. 19 of the present report.

Source: Excerpt from *General and Complete Disarmament: Transparency in Armaments, Report on the Register of Conventional Arms, Report of the Secretary-General,* UN General Assembly document A/47/342, 14 Aug. 1992, pp. 8–29.

THE UN REGISTER OF CONVENTIONAL ARMS: A NEW INSTRUMENT FOR COOPERATIVE SECURITY

Hendrik Wagenmakers

. . .

Basic Elements of the Register

The UN register is intended to establish a universal and non-discriminatory repository of data and information, which will be maintained at UN headquarters in New York. It is to include data on international arms transfers as well as information provided by member states on their relevant policies, military holdings and arms procurement through national production. Eventually the register is intended to expand into other categories of information, so the resolution also establishes a group of government experts to meet in 1994 to evaluate the first two years of the register process and consider its further development.

The basic elements of the register contained in the original resolution were adjusted by a panel of technical experts under my chairmanship. Member states are requested to submit data, and, if available, background information, by April 30 each year on the number of items exported to or imported from any other country during the previous year. . . .

. . .

. . . The focus is on weapons indispensable for surprise attacks and large-scale offensive military actions. These weapons systems are relatively easy to identify, define, record and monitor.

Information is supplied to the register on a voluntary basis. And while the register has no monitoring capability, states are free to take up their concerns in bilateral discussions based on the data and information the register provides.

Potential for Success

As part of the wider transparency process, the register is founded on the long-standing basic principles of cooperative security among states. These principles include cooperative international security as a means to maintain international peace and security, in conformity with the UN Charter; the inherent right of self-defense; preservation of regional peace, security and stability (and the concept of reasonable defense to ensure that security); undiminished security for all states at the lowest possible level of armaments; recognition of the legitimacy of conventional arms transfers to meet the security and defense needs of UN member states; and responsibility on the part of both supplier and recipient states to exercise due restraint in exports and imports.

The 1991 EC–Japanese proposal to the UN General Assembly for a conventional arms register did not come as a bolt from the blue. In 1978, at about the same time the United States and the Soviet Union were engaged in talks on limiting conventional arms transfers, the 10th special session of the General Assembly urged major arms suppliers and recipient countries to consult on ways to limit the international transfer of all types of conventional arms. In addition, the heads of state or government of the non-aligned countries stressed in their 1989 Belgrade summit that "The issue of international arms transfers should be addressed in conjunction with the question of reducing international tensions, enhancing confidence, promoting the peaceful settlement of conflicts, checking the arms race and realizing disarmament under effective international control." A similar call was made in 1992 at the non-aligned movement's summit in Jakarta, which stressed the urgent need to curb the development and excessive build-up of conventional and all other kinds of armaments. Other initiatives in support of an arms register have come from virtually every region of the world, including the Organization of American States, the European Council and the Conference on Security and Cooperation in Europe (CSCE).

Reporting Procedures

The reporting procedures of the UN register are designed to achieve the goals of non-discrimination and universality. The one-page standardized reporting form is easy to fill out, underscoring the register's practicality and the desire to convince states to submit data in the most transparent mode possible. . . .

In contrast to similar reporting exercises, the register is designed for verification through cross-checking: the report returned by one state should match that of the other involved in a reported transfer. Moreover, the computerized database of the UN Office for Disarmament Affairs (ODA) holds out the prospect of maximizing access to register information by member states, either through on-line (electronic) connection or by transferring computer information storage disks. The information will become available to the public in an annual report from the secretary-general.

It is with a view to fulfilling the same objective of consistency of information that the General Assembly has recommended that member states should, effective immediately, provide the secretary-general with background information on their relevant military policies and holdings and their procurement of conventional arms through national production (preferably together with their reports on international arms transfers). No special reports need to be prepared for submission to the register; states can draw directly on previously published government information, including such items as white papers and policy statements.

A Family of Efforts

As it is currently designed, the register uses a "building block" approach; it is a first step toward a more comprehensive system of cooperative security that works in concert with many other efforts, incorporating formal and informal arrangements among states in a mutually reinforcing way. As envisioned by the General Assembly and supported by the Security Council heads of state in their summit declaration of January 31, 1992, the concept transcends the mere registration of arms transfers. . . .

The resolution that established the register of conventional arms invited all UN member states to take parallel measures on a national, regional and global basis to promote openness and transparency in armaments. Governments are also invited to inform the secretary-general of their arms import and export policies, legislation and administrative procedures, and are doing so.

One additional benefit of the register approach is the increasing attention governments are giving to cooperative efforts to halt illicit arms trade, which often has disproportionately large consequences for international security. Illegally transferred arms, even small arms, may under certain circumstances, such as Somalia, undermine the internal security and socioeconomic development of affected states. And while it is not part of the work of the register, this issue is being dealt with in parallel by the UN Disarmament Commission (UNDC), which is scheduled to take up this matter in its 1993 session.
. . .
Separate from the UN system, but

also working in concert to achieve the same goals, the transparency process is stimulated by agreements on a regional scale, such as the confidence-building and security measures adopted by the CSCE signatory states, the exchanges of information under the CFE and the Open Skies Treaties. Similar efforts are underway in other regions: in Asia, there is the important Treaty of Amity and Cooperation in Southeast Asia, which was endorsed by the General Assembly last year as providing "a strong foundation for regional confidence-building and for regional cooperation." Similar signs of consensus and cooperation are expressed in a recent declaration of the Organization of American States.

Other examples of the trend toward greater transparency can be found in the Declaration on Non-Proliferation and Arms Exports adopted by the European Council in Luxembourg in June 1991, and the firm commitment to the UN register expressed by the CSCE council in its Prague declaration of January 1992. Moreover, the Vienna Forum for Security Cooperation has recently agreed to exchange copies of national submissions to the UN register among themselves. . . . Over the long term, and recognizing the current difficulty in distinguishing between defensive and provocative arms transfers, it is possible to envision formal regional agreements on what constitutes clearly excessive or destabilizing conventional military capabilities.

Strengths and Benefits

. . . Any assessment of the register process, as it has evolved more recently, must take into account a number of genuine benefits to the international community.

One of these benefits, previously mentioned, is the consensus which has emerged in support of the register. Its creation has provided the international community a focal point for discussions on the benefits of transparency, and has

given states from all geopolitical quarters an opportunity to fashion realistic approaches that link open dissemination of military information with the larger questions of international peace and security.

The register has produced a cross checking form of verification through which states can compare declared data with other register data and with information from external sources. Questions can then be raised, not by an independent body, which may be perceived as discriminatory, but by the member states themselves, thereby respecting the basic sovereignty of states and optimizing the likelihood that states will continue to participate. In fact, at the regional level, incremental consultative and cooperative moves are already noticeable; for example, CSCE has started to do this.

The register will not only lead to transparency at the international level but also has the potential to foster transparency within member states. During our panel discussions it became clear that in some cases national laws and procedures have still to be drawn up. In other cases they may have to be changed, in the direction of more openness, if states are to report arms transfer data and background information to the register. . . . Also, much of the arms trade involves proprietary commercial information, meaning that states will have to provide information heretofore hidden by international industrial practices. While it is too early to make firm predictions, it is possible to imagine a time soon when this side benefit will be widely recognized.

Even if it is debatable whether these returns will provide a significant net increase in knowledge about the flow of weapons and who has how much of what, there is still the key point that for the first time, governments will submit official, accountable data to other governments via the register. Yet at the same time, no military secrets are compromised; to a certain extent the information to be reported has already been made public by professional non-government organizations like the International Institute for Strategic Studies and the Stockholm International Peace Research Institute. The difference is that the register will contain official government information that can then be used for consultations between states. This official information represents the first building block for the reduction of armaments, which will be required in order to accomplish the important objectives of stability, peace and security at the lowest possible level of armaments. Under UN rules, no information from non-governmental sources can be introduced into official debates, and the information on the register solves this problem as well.

Finally, the United Nations has begun to revamp the way that it has traditionally dealt with disarmament issues during the Cold War. In its fall 1992 session, the First Committee of the General Assembly received a major report from the secretary-general, entitled *New Dimensions of Arms Regulation and Disarmament in the Post-Cold War Era.* In March 1993, a first-ever "resumed session" of the First Committee of the UN General Assembly reconvened for the express purpose of addressing the suggestions made by the secretary-general and strengthening the United Nation's disarmament armament machinery. In all of these deliberations, the register has served as the primary example of the post-Cold War thinking mentioned earlier, and because it is a formal instrument now in place, it is viewed as one of the models for efforts by states and regional organizations to establish confidence-building measures linked to peace, security, arms reduction and disarmament.

Expanding the Register in 1994

The resolution establishing the register requests the secretary-general to appoint in 1994 a group of governmental experts to prepare a report on the continuing operation of the register and its further development. By May 1994, the UN Register of Conventional Arms will have accumulated two years of data and background information on conventional arms transfers, providing the group of governmental experts assembled that year with a starting point for their work. By then, we will know more about the register in the practical sense, and will begin to have answers to such questions as how many member states have returned the standardized reporting form, what other information they provided, whether the standardized reporting form is satisfactory, how the information is being handled and compiled by the United Nations, and to what extent the register is being consulted by UN member states.

The 1994 group of governmental experts will also have to evaluate the register in a more conceptual sense to determine to what extent it has contributed, as a first step, to an enhanced level of transparency in armaments, and thereby to confidence-building, early warning and international security. The group will also look at what can be done to further develop and expand the register.

The agenda for the work of the group will certainly focus on these questions, and quite likely will include other items as well. In taking a critical look at the extent and nature of participation by member states and the usefulness of the standardized reporting form, the panel will have to ensure that if it proves necessary, no measure is left undone to increase participation and to improve the submission of data and information. Moreover, it is already clear that much work will be necessary to resolve definitional problems, notably the development of a common terminology pertaining to the description of international arms transfers, as well as those pertaining to other agenda items. The governmental experts panel will also do well to consider modifying the existing parameters of the seven categories of conventional arms.

One could also envision the inclusion of entirely new categories of conventional military items . . . .

It is important to stress, however, that the addition of new categories should not compromise prospects of ensuring the widest possible participation in the register. A key principle for adding categories should be their military relevance in terms of the significance of their impact on regional and global stability. Moreover, arms sales nowadays often involve components and subsystems, and reporting on these might become a complicating factor. There are limits to just how far it is possible to scale down or disaggregate items to be reported without making the process incredibly cumbersome and without increasing the risk of not seeing the forest for the trees.

As to the inclusion of data on military holdings and procurement through national production, full and open disclosure in this category would go a long way toward alleviating concerns of various states about the overall military capabilities and military production of their neighbors or other states in the region. This issue is highly relevant in the efforts to eliminate possible inequalities between importing states and those whose arms requirements are met entirely from indigenous production—inequalities that can severely strain regional power balances and national sense of security. History has shown that spiraling arms races are invariably sparked by a perceived imbalance of power among rival states. This was an issue during the debate on the General Assembly resolution, and the 150 states that agreed to start the transparency process by registering arms transfers will be looking for the early addition or inclusion of military holdings and procure-

ment data to the register process. This inclusion was an especially important point for states currently involved with, or threatened by, potential regional conflicts.

Weapons of Mass Destruction

The UN resolution specifically mandates that the transparency process also address weapons of mass destruction. Providing data and information on these weapons clearly widens the scope of the transparency exercise beyond registering conventional arms transfers. The basic idea, inherent in the building block approach to reaching the goals set forth by the General Assembly, is that the register will, in due course, contain data and information on military outlays as well as aggregate military force structures and figures, and will include weapons of mass destruction. This is certainly a long-term project. On the other hand, a good deal of information on nuclear holdings is already in the public domain. For instance, treaties like START I and START II are routinely issued as documents of the Conference on Disarmament, thus ensuring wide dissemination of information on strategic nuclear arsenals and weapons.

Several highly effective treaty groups and organizations are already involved in creating a climate that enhances the principles of information sharing and transparency, both in terms of conventional and nuclear forces and between non-nuclear weapon-states and nuclear-weapon states. This is especially true of the almost universal adherence to the nuclear Non-Proliferation Treaty and the related International Atomic Energy Agency (IAEA) safeguards system. In addition, regional arrangements like the Euratom treaty and the nuclear weapon-free zones established by the recently reinforced Tlatelolco and Rarotonga treaties, are invaluable mechanisms for creating a general environment of cooperative security and trust. The same holds true for the new Chemical Weapons Convention, whose effective verification provisions should lead to total transparency. Similarly, the attempts to create a binding verification mechanism for the Biological Weapons Convention bode well for the future. Each of these are positive advancements that are fully consonant with the spirit of the General Assembly resolution, which specified that transparency in implementing the register must be developed in accordance with existing legal instruments.

Transparency and High Technology

UN General Assembly Resolution 46/36 L also mentions the transfer of high technology items and systems with military applications as one of the areas to be dealt with in the transparency process. . . .

Universal compliance with effectively verifiable non-proliferation agreements would greatly facilitate meaningful dialogue within the community of states. There are encouraging signs in some regions where, until recently, the already existing norms and agreements were not fully observed. For instance, some 30 important suppliers from highly industrialized countries as well as developing countries are complying, *de jure* or *de facto,* with the Missile Technology Control Regime (MTCR). It seems the time has come when new approaches could be explored that run parallel with those based primarily or solely on restrictions and on technology denial.

Related to this, however, is the fact that an effective transparency regime can, over time, prove to be the key to a transition from the "denial approach" to "conditioned access" to necessary armaments for self-defense. The MTCR is, for the most part, a classic "access denial" approach to a specific problem, while the NPT is an illustration of "conditioned access." It is this notion of conditioned access, coupled with self-

restraint, that ultimately provides the best model in the long run if we are to achieve freedom of access for all states to technology that enhances their development, while taking into account the often competing impulses of respect for commercial enterprise and proprietary rights on the one hand, and respect for the principles of non-proliferation on the other.

Prognosis for Expansion

While all this sounds rather optimistic, we must bear in mind that the development of the register into a universal, comprehensive confidence-building instrument is a gradual process. The register deals with arms and armament, indispensable instruments to ensure national security, which is at the heart of the policies of any responsible government. It is therefore vital that member states be convinced that whatever information they disclose is consonant with national security considerations. Indeed, they should feel that their security is enhanced by participation in the register. . . . Undeniably, the military plays a key role in many developing countries as a nation-building instrument, often in ways that are partly psychological and non-quantifiable. But the advantages of putting a halt to wasteful and basically unaffordable arms races and of concentrating scarce resources on socioeconomic development are too obvious for the register not to be given its proper chance.

Certainly, as mentioned earlier, the process will take time, and realistic assessments of the potential for success must always take into account a world rife with regional and ethnic conflicts. Even without such bloody confrontations, it took the states participating in the CSCE nearly 20 years to come to a stage where the seemingly endless talks finally yielded concrete, binding measures. Additionally, some states may view the register, not as a floor or first building block, but as a ceiling—the minimum effort that may make reductions in arms unnecessary. Such risks are real, given the fact that this approach is still in its infant stages. But the openness of the process and the consensus that has developed around it could work to gradually change such attitudes. . . .

Conclusion

It seems increasingly clear that transparency is a process which has a clearly defined future. A wide spectrum of efforts, consisting of formal and informal approaches within and outside the UN system, and at international, regional and subregional levels, is well underway. As a constituent part of this process, the UN Register of Conventional Arms, through its intrinsic value and thanks to parallel endeavors, can be highly effective in helping to reduce dangerous misperceptions as well as to promote trust and partnership between states. It is clearly in the best interests of UN member states to take advantage of this new vehicle to enhance their security, at no economic cost.

In practical terms, the register might eventually be enhanced by some form of consultative mechanism, whereby common analysis of the information provided to the register would help participants develop clearer understandings of each other's view of how security is affected by arms acquisitions. It would most likely also provide a starting point for an exchange of views on cases where excessive buildups might be developing or be seen as developing without sufficient explanation.

In the absence of such a consultative mechanism, it is to be hoped that in the near future the practice of bilateral consultation on the basis of data and information provided to the register would be a starting point for effective bilateral communication. . . .

The transparency exercise and the arms register combine to offer a viable and effective mechanism for achieving greater national and international security. Obviously this will depend on the good will of member states and their willingness to comply with the spirit as well as the letter of the resolution. Certainly the course ahead is not without major pitfalls and potential blockades, nor is the arms register an end in itself. But by establishing the UN register, the international community has created a unique confidence-building and early warning tool that has great potential if states are prepared to contribute to, and use it.

Source: Excerpt from an article published in *Arms Control Today*, Apr. 1993, pp. 16–21.

THE UN REGISTER OF CONVENTIONAL ARMS: RATIONALES AND PROSPECTS FOR COMPLIANCE AND EFFECTIVENESS

Edward J. Laurance

. . .

Rationales and Prospects for Compliance

. . .

The first reason why many states will submit data is basic inertia. . . . [E]very step in the process has been carefully crafted so that the concerns of the maximum number of states are taken into account. Further steps are being planned, such as regional workshops prior to the submission date of April 30, 1993, to assist those states that desire to submit data. And this momentum has been rooted in realism and universality: all the states have refused to develop yet another sterile exercise so typical of the UN during the Cold War. A price has been paid for such support, namely a process that is very incremental. The first step, reporting arms transfers in seven categories of conventional weapons, is a small one. Yet the momentum is there. . . .

But there are more substantive rationales for compliance. Some states in Europe (e.g., Italy) have domestic laws and policies that call for maximum transparency of arms data. These states will go far beyond the minimum transparency required, perhaps even including the financial arrangements of arms deals. In effect, actual submissions will begin to empirically define the concept of transparency. Much of the information to be reported has already been made public, if not by governments then by outside groups such as the International Institute for Strategic Studies and the Stockholm International Peace Research Institute. On the other hand, there are many states that not only do not practice such transparency at home but have laws that forbid such disclosure. This could be a barrier to reporting. Or, faced with the momentum and other advantages of international transparency, states may wish to change their domestic environment. The result would be a further increase in international transparency, beyond that achieved by the register. States that have long hoped for transparency on the part of their neighbors may go along with the register just to see if such a result may be forthcoming.

It should also be noted that reporting arms exports and imports, particularly for the first two years, presents minimal security risks for most states. Most of the data are public, and for the very sensitive transfers varying levels of transparency can be applied. The East–West dimension has disappeared and the international system is at a point where few conflicts are likely to be directly and immediately affected in a major way by arms transfers in the categories covered by the register. The next few years appear to provide a window of opportunity for such an experiment. It should also be

remembered that for many states the control envisioned by many. In the wake of the Iraqi invasion of Kuwait, the calls for arms trade control were many. States tightened up their export control systems, U.S. president George Bush called for control of arms exports to the Middle East, and the five largest arms exporting states began to discuss such control. When the rest of the world began to respond positively and indicate that this might be a good idea, the concept of the register began to take concrete shape. Recipients, traditionally worried about a northern conspiracy to deprive them of their right to national security, found the idea of a register a safer response to the Iraq situation. Suppliers, suddenly besieged by protests from their arms industries at the thought of arms export controls, also saw some comfort in the idea of the register as a first step. The above logic would seem to be that, rather than risk a failed register that might see more extreme control proposals resurface, many states will comply with this first incremental step.

Throughout the development of the register, the question arose as to how to deal with illegal arms transfers. The answer was always the same, that the register was about *legal* arms trade. In a very important way the register legitimizes the arms trade. It is not a *control* mechanism, and although the resolution expresses the hope that through transparency states may achieve security at the "lowest possible level of armaments," reduction of the arms trade is not the register's primary purpose. States submitting data are in effect saying that they do not view their exports and imports as destabilizing. Failure to report may have the opposite connotation. In addition, there is no verification mechanism for the register, save the fact that the identical arms transfer has to be reported by both the importer and exporter states. This creates a situation in which a state hesitant to report an arms transfer may be faced with the state at the other end of the deal reporting, thereby creating further incentives to report. . . .

During the original debate many states complained that a register that reported only arms transfers would be discriminatory. Their concerns were taken into account by the provision of a formal agenda for a 1994 panel that would discuss expanding the register to request states to submit data on additional categories of equipment, procurement through national production, military inventories, weapons of mass destruction, and the transfer of military technology. In the second half of their report the panel made this agenda more specific. It now includes the possibility of expanding existing categories by modifying parameters or introducing new ones and introducing new categories. Items to be discussed for inclusion in the register in 1994 include aerial refueling, reconnaissance and electronic warfare aircraft, ground-to-air missiles, precision-guided munitions, cluster bombs, and fuel-air explosives. Assuming that these states were sincere in their desire to have universal and nondiscriminatory transparency, they would have a strong incentive to submit the requested data during the first two years of the register to see if the world is serious about taking their concerns into account. Lack of participation in the register by these states would provide powerful evidence for the nay-sayers who felt that the whole exercise was just more or the same rhetorical approach to international security problems.

Rationales for Noncompliance

Some states may be very reluctant to be completely transparent for security reasons. Political culture and attitudes toward secrecy in national security matters will be a very important obstacle for some states. As indicated above, the procedures developed for the register explicitly deal with this situation. Some states will have legal obstacles, in regard both to their domestic laws and the requirement to maintain confidentiality of commercial contracts. There are ways to deal with these questions. Russia for example, has made it clear that it intends to query all of its client countries and seek permission to make public information on arms transfers covered by the register. A further reluctance may stem from the fact that if a country has once been transparent in submitting data, it will find it difficult to go in the opposite direction. This was a constant theme throughout the debate on whether a "description of item" column should be included as part of the declaration form. Without the column states would not have been in this dilemma. The consensus reached was that such a column is desirable, but it remains to be seen how states take advantage of the opportunity to increase the transparency of information on arms deals.

Some states may be waiting to see how others respond. If that is the case, the assessment of the participation and transparency levels actually achieved should cover the first two years in the aggregate, not just the first year. One can assume that the data from the first year will be well publicized and that many state-by-state assessments of compliance and transparency will quickly follow. Only when states have been given the opportunity to respond to such assessments can a valid picture emerge as to whether the register is producing the expected level of transparency.

The upheavals of the past few years have produced an additional obstacle for states reporting data on arms exports and imports. This is particularly true in the states of the former Soviet Union and Warsaw Pact. The national export control systems that would produce such data vary significantly in this part of the world. At the upper end of the scale are countries such as Poland and Hungary, which have taken major steps to control their arms industries and put export controls in place. Russia is experiencing serious problems because its central control system disappeared with the collapse of the Soviet Union and its replacement is only just taking shape. As a result, for the past year many arms deliveries have been made without the knowledge of the central national export control authorities who are responsible for reporting the data to the UN. In countries such as Ukraine, controls are practically nonexistent. At this point it would be literally impossible for Ukraine to comply with the register. It is ironic that just at that time in history when the Persian Gulf War has produced an international consensus that arms transfers can have negative consequences, a significant number of states with large arms exporting capabilities are having difficulty determining actual export levels.

. . .

Source: Excerpt from an article in *Washington Quarterly* (MIT Press), vol. 16 (spring 1993), pp. 163–72.

THE UNITED NATIONS REGISTER OF CONVENTIONAL ARMS

Herbert Wulf

. . .

II. The history of the Register and transparency in the armaments process

. . .

At the 20th session of the General Assembly in 1965, Malta submitted a draft resolution to invite the Eighteen-Nation Disarmament Committee (ENDC) to consider the transfers of arms between states.[1]

In 1968 Denmark, together with Iceland, Malta and Norway as co-sponsors, submitted a draft resolution requesting the Secretary-General to ascertain the positions of governments on contributing arms transfer data to a UN register. The proposal was not put for a vote because of opposition mainly from the non-aligned countries.

In 1976, at the 31st session of the General Assembly, 13 countries sponsored a draft resolution in which a factual study of the international transfer of conventional arms was requested. A majority voted to adjourn the debate.

In 1978 it was agreed that the United Nations should undertake a study on the subject of a register of arms transfers and control of the illicit trade in arms.[2] At the request of the General Assembly in various resolutions, the Secretary-General, with the assistance of groups of governmental experts, carried out several studies on arms transfers and related issues.[3]

[1] The proposal was rejected by a vote of 18 in favour with 19 against and 39 abstentions. For the history and a review of previous proposals for an arms transfer register, see UNGeneral Assembly, *Report by the Secretary-General, Study on Ways and Means of Promoting Transparency in International Transfers of Conventional Arms,* UN document A/46/301, 9 Sep. 1991, pp. 16–17; and Corradini, A., *Considerations of the Question of International Arms Transfers by the United Nations,* Disarmament Topical Papers 3 (UN: New York, 1990), pp. 44–59.

[2] United Nations General Assembly Resolution S-10/2.

[3] UN, *Relationship between Disarmament and Development* (UN document A/36/356); *Comprehensive Study on Confidence-Building Measures* (A/36/474); *Relationship between Disarmament and International Security* (A/36/597); *Economic and Social Consequences of the Arms Race and Military Expenditures* (A/8469/Rev.1, A/32/88/Rev.1, A/37/386, A/43/368); *Study on Conventional*

While a number of these studies requested the establishment of a United Nations conventional arms transfer register, there was no agreement on joint action until 1991. The main reason why a number of developing countries rejected the arms transfer register was its claimed partiality. Critics rightly pointed out that in a transfer register recipient countries without domestic arms production facilities would have to report all their arms imports, while the major arms producers would not have to report much at all. Such a one-sided register would over a long period of time have given a fairly detailed picture of the weapon inventory of the importing countries, while the major arms-producing countries could continue to conceal their weapon inventories. Consequently, governments of the developing countries asked to establish a more comprehensive register which would include both transfers and production of arms, but no compromise was reached.

One reason for the reservations on the part of some Western countries, particularly the US Government, was their belief that some of the proposed controls of arms transfers were perceived as not desirable, while desirable controls (that is, on Soviet arms exports) were non-negotiable. In addition, the Register was seen as a rhetorical exercise with little or no relevance to real arms control. Only when it became apparent that the Register would be approved by the UN in 1991 did the US Government join the group of co-sponsors and support it.

III. The 1991 UN General Assembly decision

Although the overwhelming majority which voted for the establishment of the Register seems to signal a consensus

that had failed so often before, the debate among the UN member states indicates that many governments were not entirely satisfied with the resolution.[1]

To reach agreement, in contrast to the result of previous efforts, one important alteration had to be made in the resolution sponsored by Japan and co-sponsored by Western countries.[2] In addition to information on the export and import of conventional arms, countries are also invited to provide information 'on military holdings, procurement through national production and relevant policies'.[3] . . .

. . .

Despite this compromise to accommodate some of the complaints of member states, many government representatives voiced reservations. Before the vote was taken, the Cuban delegate raised the often mentioned criticism of partiality and pointed out that his government was not satisfied with just the possibility for expansion: 'What we are against is the establishment of a partial and selective registry which relates only to international transfers of conventional weapons and not to production and stockpiling, to the transfer of advanced military technology, to research and development activities or to weapons of

---

[1] Moodie, M., 'Transparency in armaments: a new item for the new security agenda', *Washington Quarterly*, summer 1992, pp. 75–82, accurately depicts the opposition to the UN First Committee version of the original resolution by such countries as Argentina, Brazil, Egypt and Pakistan.

[2] The minutes of the debate in the First Committee of the 46th session of the General Assembly (UN document A/C.1/46/PV.37), pp. 18–22, show that last-minute revisions were introduced into the draft resolution to comply with some of the requests of countries in favour of an expanded register.

[3] Paragraph 7 of General Assembly Resolution 46/36 L, UN General Assembly document A/RES/46/36 L, 9 Dec. 1991.

Disarmament (A/39/348); *Study on All Aspects of Regional Disarmament* (A/35/416); *Reduction of Military Budgets* (A/35/479, A/S-12/7, A/40/421).

mass destruction.'[1] After the vote several delegates stated for the record their continued reservations.[2] Their criticism concentrated on the following issues:

1. Indigenous production capabilities and advanced production technology need to be taken into account simultaneously with arms transfers (Algeria, North Korea, Pakistan and Uganda).

2. The national security interests of member states have to be taken into consideration (Pakistan and Singapore).

3. All types of weapons, particularly those with more devastating effects (weapons of mass destruction), need to be included (Algeria, Iran and Syria).

The background to these statements for the UN record are, of course, often regional conflicts. Pakistan, for example, would want Indian arms production to be registered; North Korea would want South Korean production registered; and Algeria, Iran and Syria want regional chemical and nuclear arsenals registered, particularly Israel's nuclear weapons. This suggests that the agenda of disagreement is as much regional and South–South as it is North–South disagreement. What effect this will have on the 1994 review is uncertain.

IV. Technical procedures

. . .

. . . The differences of opinion on the function and content of the Register that had emerged during the General Assembly debate continued to dominate the deliberations of the Panel—although the report was approved by consensus. The divergencies are illustrative, as they indicate how governments view the purpose and the future of the Register. They are summarized in the sections below.

The mandate of the Panel

Differences first emerged in interpreting the mandate of the Panel. While a number of Panel members (most outspokenly those from China and Egypt but also those from most of the other developing countries) suggested making adjustments to the seven categories of weapon system in the General Assembly resolution by defining the weapons and adding to them, a narrower interpretation was favoured by others (most decisively by France, the UK and the USA). They suggested sticking as closely as possible to the text of the resolution and insisted that it was not the mandate of the Panel to add other categories of weapon system (neither conventional nor weapons of mass destruction nor production technology). As can be seen by comparing the original seven categories described in the 1991 General Assembly resolution with the definitions as adjusted by the Panel,[3] the Panel made some changes but did not add new categories of weapon or production technology. In the compromise reached, the Panel decided to leave this issue for the 1994 Register review.

. . .

Adjustment and definitions of weapon categories

Agreement about the exact definitions

---

[1] Statements by Member States in the 46th session of the General Assembly (UN document A/46/PV.66, Agenda Item 60), p. 43.

[2] Among them were (in chronological order) Pakistan, North Korea, Algeria, Iran, Singapore, Syria and Uganda. See Statement by Member States in the 46th session of the General Assembly, UN document A/46/PV.66, Agenda Item 60, pp. 47–55. In addition, the representative of Lithuania stated that his country might not be able to fulfil the requirements of the Register since a considerable number of Soviet forces were still stationed in Lithuania without the agreement or consent of his government.

[3] The Annex of Resolution 46/36 L has been revised. The revised version (Resolution 47/342, appears in UN Secretary-General, *Report on the Register of Conventional Arms*, UN document A/47/342, 14 Aug. 1992.

was problematic for some of the weapon categories. A consensus report could only be achieved by many compromises until the very last day of the five weeks of deliberations. The most critical disagreements were the following:[1]

Combat aircraft (category IV) and *attack helicopters* (category V). The Chinese member of the Panel (with varying degrees of support from several others) suggested adding to the combat aircraft category reconnaissance and electronic warfare aircraft, air-refuelling aircraft, command and early-warning aircraft. The reasoning was that such aircraft could add considerable offensive capabilities to the armed forces and should thus be reported. These proposals were rejected until a last-minute compromise was found to include versions of combat aircraft 'which perform specialized electronic warfare, suppression of air defence or reconnaissance missions'. In other words, not all but *versions of combat aircraft* for reconnaissance and electronic warfare are included and air-refuelling aircraft are excluded. A similar compromise was found for attack helicopters.

Warships (category VI). The original definition gives a displacement of 850 metric tonnes as a minimum level for reporting. At the suggestion of the Malaysian member of the Panel, the displacement was lowered to 750 metric tonnes to include certain types of corvette. An important category of highly effective ships, fast attack missile craft, which usually have a displacement of about 250 tonnes or less would thus not be included in the Register. These warships are transferred in larger num-

bers than the heavier ships of 750 tonnes and more. It was much more difficult to reach agreement to include fast missile attack craft. The British member of the Panel (with support from the USA) argued that the important point was to report the missiles (which had to be done under category VII). The ships could be considered as a missile platform. A majority of the Panel favoured the inclusion of this type of ship. It was agreed to include ships 'with a standard displacement of less than 750 metric tonnes, equipped for launching missiles with a range of at least 25 kilometres or torpedoes with similar range'. This adjustment to a weapon category was the most far-reaching adjustment made by the Panel.

Missiles and missile launchers (category VII). Two issues were of major concern in this category. First, China suggested excluding all missiles of a defensive nature, particularly surface-to-air missiles. The categorization of weapon systems as offensive or defensive caused difficulties and differing opinions within the Panel, as in many other forums. After long debates and as part of a general compromise, the Panel accepted the exclusion of all 'ground-to-air missiles',[2] on the basis that these missiles were used for defensive purposes and that not many ground-to-air missiles had a range of 25 kilometres or more.

Second, and more importantly, a long debate emerged on the issue of whether missiles and missile launchers were to be reported in one single figure. It was clear to the panelists that this was like 'adding apples and pears'. Nevertheless, the countries who insisted on this, particularly the United Kingdom and the United States, were not willing to accept the disaggregation of missiles and missile launchers. In contrast to the rest of

---

[1] For other, less important changes, compare the original definitions of the 7 weapon categories and the revised versions. Both are printed in UN Secretary-General, *Report on the Register of Conventional Arms*, UN document A/47/342, 14 Aug. 1992, pp. 11–12 (revised) and pp. 25–26 (original).

---

[2] Note that not all surface-to-air missiles (SAMs) are excluded; SAMs mounted on ships are to be reported.

the report, an example is given (in paragraph 16a) to explain this unusual way of reporting: 'For example, if a country imports six missile launchers and 100 associated missiles as well as 500 missiles associated with other launchers covered under categories I to VI, the number 606 will be entered.' One hundred missiles of one type plus 500 missiles of another type plus 6 missile launchers make a total of 606 'items', but it is unclear how each is defined. . . .

Designations of weapon systems

The most divergent views were expressed on whether or not weapon designations would have to be mandatory in the report. The consequences of this decision have important implications for the value of the Register. The alternative was the following. If all transfers in one category, for example combat aircraft, are lumped into a single figure when a country reports its exports to another country, it would be left to the reader of the Register to speculate which aircraft might have been transferred. If designations or descriptions of the combat aircraft are reported, the observer will have information about the particular sale and can distinguish between modern, technically advanced and often expensive aircraft on the one hand and cheap, simple, often second-hand equipment on the other. The Brazilian and Italian members of the Panel and others argued that it is the opposite of transparency to treat a light attack aircraft, armed with a machine-gun and with a limited radius of operation, in the same way as a modern, missile-carrying, multi-purpose fighter.

A similar argument was made about whether a remarks column should be provided to allow governments to explain a particular import or export.

While many developing countries had reservations against the establishment of the Register in the first place, once it was established this group of delegates pleaded for detailed reporting to make the Register a valuable instrument of transparency. In contrast, several members from the industrialized countries argued that—in addition to reasons of national security—it was necessary to have a simple system of reporting to make the Register a success. Reporting should be as simple as possible to allow all countries to participate.

The compromise found at the suggestion of the Brazilian, Canadian and Italian Panel members is clearly reflected in the reporting forms . . . Two remarks columns—separated by a small margin from the other columns—are placed at the right side of both the import and the export forms. This graphic separation of the data is intended to make clear that information in this column is not only voluntary but, as one member phrased it during the deliberations, 'very voluntary'. . . .

. . .

V. The objectives of the Register and the prospects for implementation

Compared to the wider goals of enhancing peace and stability, increasing openness, transparency and confidence, and supporting the restraint in arms imports and exports, the first step of the Register is a very modest one. In judging the relevance of the Register, however, it should be observed that international arms transfers were a taboo subject for a long time, and the concept of the registration of conventional armaments was considered to be a 'non-starter' in the United Nations.[1] The Register is none the less a modest step for several rea-

---

[1] This conclusion was drawn by the former UN Under-Secretary General for Disarmament Affairs, Yasushi Akashi, 'An overview of the situation', *Transparency in International Arms Transfers*, Disarmament Topical Papers 3 (United Nations: New York, 1990), p. 3.

sons.

1. In its present form the Register will not significantly facilitate a judgement about the military capabilities of countries which contribute to it. In addition to the treatment of arms production capabilities, there is no obligation to report on an entire range of weapons: small arms, bombs, munition, mortars, guns below a certain calibre, missiles below a range of 25 kilometres, support ships, non-combat planes and helicopters, and others. Moreover, many other forms of arms-related trade are outside the scope of the Register, including major subsystems (especially engine and electronic upgrades), dual-use items and production technologies.

The Register will be of no assistance in understanding the economics of the arms trade since the value of given transactions and the details of their financing are outside its scope.

2. The Register and its aim of transparency are not synonymous with a restriction on arms and were not intended to be. Whether the Register will be an 'action-oriented tool' and an 'instrument of preventive diplomacy', in the words of the Secretary-General in his foreword to the report,[1] has to be proven in practice. In the aftermath of Iraq's invasion of Kuwait, the calls by many governments for arms trade control and tightening of export control systems went far beyond the goals of the Register. However, the Register was deliberately never intended to establish a new control mechanism, and reduction of the arms trade is not the primary purpose of the Register.

3. There is no verification mechanism. It is a voluntary exercise of member states which will not be controlled or verified. The Panel of Governmental Technical Experts made it clear that the

task of the UN Secretariat is to file and distribute the incoming reports from member states but not to check or verify them. This shortcoming should, however, not be overestimated since, if importers and exporters report separately on the same deal, this will provide a signal of a discrepancy and a reference-point for cross-checking. Furthermore, the research community will certainly thoroughly scrutinize the reports of the first two years.

. . .

___

Source: Excerpt from *SIPRI Yearbook 1993: World Armaments and Disarmament* (Oxford University Press: Oxford, 1993), appendix 10F, pp. 533–44.

IMPLEMENTING AND DEVELOPING THE UNITED NATIONS REGISTER OF CONVENTIONAL ARMS

Malcolm Chalmers and Owen Greene

. . .

4. The significance of transparency

The UN Arms Register is only one example of a broader family of measures, often collectively known as transparency measures. In this chapter we examine the experience of such measures and draw some lessons that may be of relevance to the Register.

Transparency has been defined as the 'systematic provision of information on specific aspects of activities in the military field under informal or formal international arrangements.'[2] . . . [T]he potential for such arrangements was perhaps first recognised in the aftermath of World War I, when it was agreed to set up a League of Nations office respon-

___

[1] UN Secretary-General, *Report on the Register of Conventional Arms*, UN document A/47/342, 14 Aug. 1992, pp. 2–3.

[2] United Nations, Study on ways and means of promoting transparency in international transfers of conventional arms, A/46/301, September 1991, p. 13.

sible for receiving, and then publishing, copies of all arms export licences. Between 1924 and 1938, the League published 15 volumes of the Armament Yearbook, containing summaries of the strength and equipment of national armed forces. In addition, the Statistical Yearbook of the League of Nations published annual figures on the values of arms exports and imports, albeit incomplete and not based on common reporting rules.[1]

Transparency measures were also a significant part of arms control during the latter part of the cold war, particularly in Europe. Some of these measures were independent of force limitations, notably the information exchange provisions of the 1972 Agreement on Incidents at Sea and the confidence-building measures included in the 1975 Helsinki Final Act. In 1986, all members of the CSCE agreed to the Stockholm Agreement on confidence and security-building measures,[2] and in 1992 the Vienna Agreement strengthened these measures further. A second group were those associated with co-operative attempts to help verify compliance with arms limitation treaties. Perhaps the most far-reaching development in military transparency ever agreed came about as a result of the series of measures associated with the Treaty on Conventional Forces in Europe (CFE), which entered into force on 17 July 1992. In addition to limiting the size of the conventional arsenals of its 30 signatories, the Treaty requires all countries to provide annual statements to other signatories on the number, type and location of its tanks, artillery, armoured fighting vehicles, combat aircraft and combat helicopters. The first exchange of such information took place on 15 December 1992, with only Azerbaijan failing to make a return.[3]

With the end of the Cold War, the exclusion of 'non-aligned' states from European arms control has come to be seen as increasingly anachronistic. As a result, the Forum for Security Cooperation was established in September 1992 in order to bring all 53 members of the CSCE within agreed transparency regimes. In October, a number of states proposed to the Forum on Security Co-operation (FSC) that non-CFE Treaty states be asked to adhere to the CFE regimes for information exchange, verification and review. Later that month, NATO proposed that CSCE states should exchange detailed information on national defence policies, major investment projects, and defence budgets for the next five years. In November, Iceland tabled a proposal for exchange of information on non-proliferation, and it was reported that NATO would also be making a proposal on exchange of arms transfer information. And in December the EC countries suggested a military code of conduct, establishing norms for the internal conduct of military institutions.

. . .

The most important benefit of transparency is often seen as its role in reducing potentially damaging misunderstandings between states. By eroding the extent of secrecy in military affairs, transparency can, if well devised, reassure states about the peaceful and defensive intentions of others. . . .

In times of political crisis, the sort of transparency measures included in the CFE Treaty can significantly reduce the military advantage from surprise attack by making it more difficult for preparations to be made undetected. . . .

Once put into place, states cannot

---

[1] Ibid., pp. 16–17.

[2] For details of the evolution of this accord, see John Borawski, *From the Atlantic to the Urals: Negotiating Arms Control at the Stockholm Conference*, Brasseys, 1988.

[3] *Arms Control Reporter 1993*, IDDS, Cambridge MA, 1993, p. 483.

withdraw from transparency agreements—even if non-binding in nature—without attracting unwelcome scrutiny from others. . . .

One of the benefits of requiring governments to reveal military information to other states is that it will require governments to gather that information, thus helping to strengthen political control over agencies responsible for military-related activity. . . .

The government's own accountability to legislature, press and public, is in turn strengthened by a wider availability of such information. . . .

Finally, transparency regimes can also help create an environment in which negotiations to limit force levels become more acceptable. The 1986 Stockholm agreement, for example, was a significant step towards creating the verification regime that would subsequently be adopted in the CFE Treaty. Even if formal arms limitations agreements are seen as inappropriate, transparency regimes can open up new possibilities for discussing mutual restraint between potentially hostile states.

Yet attempts to create transparency regimes are not without problems, two of which it is worth highlighting here. First, there is the problem of asymmetrical openness. Any proposed regime is likely to demand greater changes for some states than others, with consequences for both its design and implementation. Second, given the selective nature of any transparency regime, there may be problems of misinterpretation should too much weight be given by policy makers to the limited information that is made available. We will discuss these two areas of possible difficulty in turn.

4.1 Asymmetrical openness

A central challenge in creating any international regime is to find means of incorporating a disparate group of states within a common framework of rules

and norms, without so diluting the content of the regime as to render it worthless. Of particular importance for transparency regimes is the difference between states that are relatively secretive or closed, in the military information they release and those which are already relatively open. . . .

One of the ways in which these competing concerns can be reconciled, at least in part, is to introduce any transparency measures in a step-by-step process rather than in a once-and-for-all, and very ambitious, agreement. . . .

Yet too gradualist an approach could mean that the benefits of transparency are unnecessarily delayed, and that the political momentum for progress may be lost. It is a matter for judgement when it is most appropriate to emphasise the benefits of an evolutionary approach, and when it would be appropriate to attempt to make more radical steps forward.

. . .

In today's more complex security environment, it will be harder to judge the best trade-off between participation and depth in transparency regimes. It may be enough to have the agreement of most states to a regime, in the expectation that others will join later, as in the Non-Proliferation Treaty. Moreover, even if states do sign up to a regime, some flexibility in the extent to which all are obliged to implement its provisions may be tolerated.

Western states can afford to take a relatively relaxed view of the military costs of transparency regimes. As democracies, they are already relatively open in discussing the detail of defence policy, though the degree of openness does vary considerably between, say, the US and the UK. Even if other states only comply partially with the requirements of transparency regimes, therefore, they are more likely to be providing information that was not previously in the public domain. The beneficiaries will include not only other countries, but also those pressing for a democratisation of security policy within these societies.

The early 1990s may offer a particularly good opportunity to push forward with the development of global transparency regimes. With the end of communism in Eastern Europe and the former Soviet Union, the demise of the military regimes that used to dominate South America, and advances also in East Asia and Africa, democratic forms of government are now more widespread than ever before. . . . Transparency agreements reached now, therefore, could help to provide a valuable means of monitoring the military activities of countries which revert to authoritarianism.

Yet the correlation between openness and democracy, while it undoubtedly exists, is not a perfect one. There may also be a perfectly understandable tendency for more vulnerable, or weaker, states to be more reticent in publishing their military strength. If the Soviet Union had been subject to recently agreed START information exchange and verification procedures in the 1950s, for example, it might well have enhanced US confidence in the first strike ability of its own strategic forces. More generally, given that militarily weak states often rely more on deceit and uncertainty to supplement real military resources than stronger ones, they may be expected to be less keen on regimes that threaten their ability to deceive. Reducing uncertainty about force sizes and deployments may reduce the ability of states to mount surprise attacks. But unless a transparency regime is appropriately designed, it might also make such an attack more likely to succeed. The need to avoid such destabilising consequences must be considered when analyzing any new proposals, and the concerns of militarily weak states on this point must be taken seriously.

Even if some initial flexibility in implementation seems an inevitable part of establishing a transparency regime that seeks to incorporate many different countries, however, there are also risks involved in too tolerant an approach to non- membership or non-compliance. Incentives for full participation need to be provided to those states who may be tempted to 'free ride', taking advantage of others' transparency while limiting their own. Serious account must be taken of the possibility of defection amongst those who have already signed up.

4.2 The dangers of misinterpretation

While some flexibility in the requirements of a transparency regime may be desirable, however, ambiguity has its dangers. States may believe that they are fulfilling the letter of data exchange agreements when others believe they are not. The consequence—as the disputes over Soviet compliance in the early 1980s demonstrated—can be increased mistrust between governments. On the other hand, it is also true that if transparency measures fail to capture the most militarily significant activities, they may contribute to a false sense of security amongst decision-makers. . . .

. . . Insofar as transparency leads to an over-emphasis on measurable and verifiable indicators of military strength, for example, it may lead to a neglect of qualitative factors: under-estimating the potential of some states and overstating that of others.

. . .

Source: Excerpt from *Peace Research Report No. 32* (Department of Peace Studies, University of Bradford, UK: Bradford, May 1993), pp. 20–27.

TRANSPARENCY IN ARMAMENTS: INFORMATION AND INTERNATIONAL SECURITY IN THE POST-COLD WAR WORLD

Ian Anthony

. . .

V. A technical evaluation of the Register

The fact that so many countries seem willing to participate in the Register is partly explained by its limited nature. The contents and reporting procedures associated with the Register were deliberately kept simple to encourage broad participation and many of the countries which participate will return nil reports stating that they had no imports or exports in any of the seven categories. In contrast to the system for standardized reporting of military expenditure—which requires considerable disaggregation of data—the Register asks countries to do very little in this regard. Many of the countries which do have imports or exports to report are likely to provide aggregate data at the minimum level of transparency required by the standardized reporting forms. Moreover, governments have been given some flexibility in deciding how to comply with even this limited request and the combination of simplicity and flexibility—while helping to achieve widespread participation—is likely to create technical problems in the early years of the Register. Solutions to these problems (some of which are noted below, though no doubt others will arise) can be outlined as an important aspect of the report on the further development of the Register to be prepared in 1994 by a group of government experts as required by resolution 46/36.

Technical problems which can be anticipated with the Register

The group of government experts which elaborated the technical procedures for the operation of the Register did not attempt to define arms transfers or rules for deciding exactly when an item was imported or exported. Governments were also left to decide on an individual basis which systems should be classified in the seven categories for the purposes of the Register. There is no detailed annex of conventional arms comparable to the Protocol on Existing Types which accompanied the CFE Treaty.

Given this national discretion it is possible that there will be some differences in interpretation on what constitutes a transfer, the timing of deliveries, whether or not certain systems fit the definition of the categories to be reported and in some cases which of the categories certain systems fit into best.[1] This section gives examples of the kind of problems which may occur.

During the establishment of the Register the question was raised whether a consultative body should cross-check returns to ensure consistency between export and import data before final reports were submitted. The idea was rejected because the self-checking verification procedure is one of the most interesting aspects of the Register. There is no procedure for retrospective modification of reports after they have been submitted to the Office for Disarmament Affairs. . . .

. . .

What is an arms transfer?

For the purposes of the Register international arms transfers involve 'in addition to the physical movement of equipment into or from national territory, the transfer of title to and control over the equipment'.[2] Therefore for the year 1992 the fact that several countries achieved their independence and with it

---

[1] During the regional workshop on Europe two participants noted that some land systems could be classified in several categories.

[2] *Report on the Register of Conventional Arms*, UN document A/47/342 (United Nations: New York 14 Aug. 1992), para 10.

'title to and control over' equipment will probably lead to the inclusion of equipment which would not normally be thought of in the same context as international arms trade. For example, Russia may well determine that equipment now in possession of the armed forces of the former Soviet Union located in newly independent countries such as Georgia and Ukraine is eligible for the UN reporting procedure. Equally, newly independent countries which emerged on the territory of the former Soviet Union and which have taken over control of armed forces with their associated equipment may want to report these to the Register precisely to underline their ownership of this equipment. This form of transfer will diminish over the next several years.

When does a delivery take place?

The final word on this belongs with governments which creates some possibility for different reporting procedures, for example if the exporter reports the export at the moment an item leaves the national territory, air or sea space but the importer reports the import when the item is inducted into the armed forces. This may happen with ships if an exporter includes a delivery when a vessel leaves the territorial waters but an importer includes a delivery when the ship is formally commissioned. It could happen with aircraft if training takes place in the exporting country before items are moved to the recipient. The exporter register an export, feeling that 'title to and control over' an aircraft has passed to the recipient even if the item is still on a training range (the recipient will certainly have to pay for any damage incurred under training). However, the recipient might register an import only when physical delivery takes place.

How should systems be classified?

As noted above there is no detailed equipment list associated with the Register categories. As a result there is the possibility that an exporter will decide to include a borderline system (for example, an armed trainer aircraft or an armed helicopter) but an importer will decide that this system does not meet the criteria laid down in the annex to the Register.

There is also a possible difficulty with deciding where to place some systems. For example, if a multiple rocket launcher fires rockets which meet the parameters of missiles and missile systems how should a report be made? Should the launcher be reported under artillery pieces, should the rockets be reported under missiles or should both be reported? Again, it is possible that an exporter will reach one conclusion and an importer another.

VI. Towards a new international information system

. . .

The support for the Register reflects a wider belief within government that an agreed body of information is necessary before political differences can be narrowed through a co-operative process based on dialogue. No such co-operative process can be expected in the immediate future as the international community is still directing most of its efforts to addressing the urgent and pressing crises in different parts of the world with more traditional tools. These crises are likely to be addressed with traditional mechanisms based on direct or indirect coercion. In the longer term, resolution 46/36 offers some indication of the elements of a more durable order capable of managing the increasingly complex international system.

The resolution indicates consensus among governments that the United Nations is one (but not the only) logical repository for comprehensive and reliable information about aspects of international security. The governments agree that this information should be stored in a manner which permits easy retrieval and distribution.[1] The resolution challenges the United Nations to evaluate fundamental issues including its attitude towards data and information and its relationship with the member States.

. . .

Resolution 46/36 does not create any exclusive function for the United Nations. On the contrary, it calls for regional and sub-regional co-operation in developing further transparency and confidence-building measures tailored to specific local conditions. Moreover, the resources of the United Nations cannot support a plan based on processing a massive volume of detailed and disaggregated data in a centralized system. As a result, a division of labour between information collection points organized on a regional basis is a necessary condition of future progress towards a global data collection and distribution system. Moreover, the UN could function as a central register of available data to which interested parties could refer. The UN could also act to facilitate data exchange, calling up requested data from the regional repository and transferring it to the customer. This would be a valuable data exchange service but it would not constitute an information system.

As presently constructed, access to the information in the Register of Conventional Arms is not restricted to governments. Whereas there is a responsibility to make information available to governments at any time on request (a privilege which only they enjoy) a consoli-

dated report will be presented to the General Assembly. This will appear as a General Assembly document, available on request. This permits the Register to act as one constituent part of an information system since data submitted on a voluntary and non-discriminatory basis by governments must be evaluated and put in context. This is a task which neither governments nor intergovernmental organizations such as the UN can perform in public. Governments are constrained in what they say about one another in public while the UN must be sensitive to the views of all of its members. No such constraints apply to the wider non-governmental community.

The power of government officials depends on their monopoly of information and there is an understandable reluctance to give this up. No doubt there will be a direct diminution in the authority of government officials as the wider distribution of information permits their judgement to be assessed in a more informed manner.

Non-government information requirements on the other hand stem from a right to evaluate the policies being made and executed on behalf of the public. Evaluations of foreign and security policy should be encouraged by the widest possible spectrum. For non-governmental consumers of information 'how much it adds to our knowledge of a particular subject' is precisely the appropriate scale against which measurement should be made.

The differences between the needs and interests of government and non-government information consumers will persist. However, the potential advantages to be gained from establishing an agreed body of information on which different consumers can draw for their specific purposes are such that they should try and reach a reasonable accommodation.

In conclusion, only when governments, international inter-governmental

---

[1] Providing a central reference system is already part of the mandate of many UN organizations. The implication of resolution 46/36 is that governments have now extended this mandate to issues of peace and security in the post-cold war political environment. Nordic Under-secretaries for Development Co-operation, *The United Nations in Development*, Final Report of the Nordic UN Project (Copenhagen/Helsinki/Oslo/Stockholm 1991), pp. 22–23.

organizations and non-government actors including the research community, the electronic and print media and other interested parties participate in a more structured exchange of information will a true information system emerge. Only when such a system emerges can a reasoned debate on the development of a rational management system for the post-cold war world begin. The UN Register of Conventional Arms represents a modest step in establishing the technical procedures on which such an information system will depend. However, its true value lies in the principles which underpin it and the process which it has initiated.

Source: Excerpt from a paper presented at the International Institute for Strategic Studies (IISS) Conference on Proliferation, Barnett Hill, UK, 5–7 May 1993.

Index